FRANCIS
FRANCO

The Times and the Man

By

Joaquín Arrarás

Translated By

J. Manuel Espinosa, Ph.D.

THE BRUCE PUBLISHING COMPANY
MILWAUKEE

Preface by the General Editor

JOAQUÍN ARRARÁS, journalist, editor, historian, has been particularly qualified for the writing of this book, both by previous training and by his intimate knowledge of events and persons described in these pages. For the past twenty years he has followed the steadily mounting career of Francisco Franco. He has enjoyed free access to unpublished official documents and valuable personal records. Minute details of important conversations and historic happenings have been secured by him from original sources.

That is one great asset of this book. The other is its strict adherence to fact, and to fact alone.

Propagandism has today become one of the world's foremost arts. Misrepresentation is paid for in precious coin. To breathe in therefore the healthy and invigorating atmosphere of this book is a bracing experience. Whether friendly or otherwise disposed, readers cannot fail to perceive that here they stand in the presence of the real Francisco Franco. To make that possible for them was the purpose in writing this work.

To say that the author, or any other writer dealing with present-day Spain, is without personal convictions on the struggle into which much of Europe and the rest of the world was dragged on one side or the other, would be an absurd contention. The point is that he has not allowed himself to be influenced unduly to the prejudice of truth. In fact he has scrupulously avoided whatever might lead to partisan discussion.

In vain, therefore, will the reader look for fiery diatribes against Fascism, Anarchism, or Communism. There is no philosophizing on the course of history. The writer remains objective. Religion is not discussed. The historic sequence inevitably called for some reference to the destruction of churches and convents, and the killing of men and women for their religious belief. But practically the only treatment of this consists in the *verbatim* citation of news items which appeared during the course of one single typical day in the government-censored press.

It is with Franco, then, that the author is concerned, with his character, his early upbringing, his entrance into the army, his thrilling adventures, his dramatic military career that made him through merit alone a captain at the age of twenty and Europe's youngest general at thirty-two. We next find him, on his return home, commissioned to establish the Spanish West Point, immediately destroyed by the new government. Quickly after this there follow the world-stirring events that now are history.

Naturally a contemporary setting was needed for the various periods in Franco's life. With bold and rapid strokes the author therefore outlines, at the different stages of his narrative, the changing conditions of the last few decades in Spain: the political troubles centering in Morocco, the bloody uprising of the Moors in their mountain fastnesses, the domestic developments at home preceding the fall of the monarchy, and all that happened thereafter.

Fortunately the author's work, in its transformation from Spanish into English, has lost none of its freshness and flavor. The velvet is still on the fruit. We have apparent here the same journalistic verve, the same vividness of narration, the same colorful descriptions and sharp-edged statement of facts. Thoroughly acquainted with conditions in Spain, Dr. Espinosa understands equally well the Spanish character and Spanish ideals. We confidently present his volume in the hope that it may clarify thought no less than convey information at this critical time.

J. H.

Contents

x CONTENTS .

CHAPTER 1

El Ferrol: Franco's Early Years

"THE port of El Ferrol has been known since ancient times as one of the best in the world, being made famous with the name 'Port of the Sun.'" William Pitt, Prime Minister of England, summed up his impression of a visit to El Ferrol with the words, "If England had a port like this, she would plate it with an armor of silver."

There is room in it for all the fleets of the world. A range of towering mountains guards it preciously, as an oyster its pearl. Its lake-smooth, placid waters extend inland for eleven miles, and from its shores are mirrored innumerable naval works and villages and summer homes, whitening the lovely and perennial verdure of its shores. They are tense, placid, and silken waters, like those of all Galician streams; waters that descended from the frozen Baltic, or that uprose, turbulent and boiling, from the Equator, and which come to rest among these towering peaks and isles to convalesce and dream of distant stars.

The Spanish government did not become aware of the real importance of El Ferrol until the eighteenth century, when the little fishing village was advanced to the rank of a Naval Base. This was in 1726. Its shores soon rang to the awakening of an industrial springtime. Docks, drydocks, shipyards, and fortresses appeared, and one after the other, in endless succession, warships, frigates, brigantines, careenage boats, and packet boats departing for the paths of war and adventure cleaved the crystal of its waters. In 1752, El Ferrol possessed the finest shipyards in the world, and provided employment for fifteen thousand workers. At one time twelve ships were built at the same time. They were dubbed by the populace with the name "The Twelve Apostles." English technicians were hired by Jorge Juan, the famous navigator, for pay which at the time seemed fabulous: a guinea a day. Of seventy-nine warships that Spain possessed in 1793, thirty-seven were anchored at El Ferrol.

The city grew up around its bay, at once its life and its glory. The memory of that fishing village was a thing of the past. The fishermen were now sailors that fought on the seven seas, holding together the remnants of the Spanish Empire that now cracked and crumbled. More and more ships sallied forth, many never to return. Spain was fighting against the fleets of half the world. Pirate ships which coveted their cargoes of American gold, hunted them; tempests lashed them cruelly. El Ferrol continued to send forth her ships. The typhoons of the Far East and the seas of the Antilles, pirate frigates, Nelson's cannon — these beckoned to them relentlessly. Rare was the day when El Ferrol was free of sorrow. For every disaster on the sea there was mourning in El Ferrol. But tradition reasserted itself with the strength of law. In the place of mariners who never came back there went forth sons or brothers.

Ill-treated by the rigors of the sea and war, El Ferrol stands out as an example of perseverance toward destiny. The sea brought it gifts and glory, just as from the sea came tragedy and ruin. For its exceptional location El Ferrol was coveted with that eagerness that draws men on to treasure. For centuries it was the greatest temptation for the ambitions of Great Britain. Once Essex and Admiral Howard sailed forth with the aim of seizing this rich Spanish port, but they were obliged to abandon their plans at the very entrance, for El Ferrol was impregnable. But England did not abandon her determination. She blockaded it, watched over it, stalked it; and in 1800 Putney sailed with fifteen thousand troops to the conquest of El Ferrol. The landing ended in tragedy. The people of El Ferrol, and perhaps Divine Providence, which keeps watch over them, decreed that the attempt should end in disaster.

The first half of the nineteenth century witnessed the decline of the power of El Ferrol. Even its promise seemed to have vanished. The poor boats of Spain were but phantoms fleeing over the seas, leaving a wake behind that seemed more like streamers of a shroud. A succession of wars, insurrections, and conspiracies had so impoverished the National Treasury that the state found it impossible to pay its employees their wages. And without wages, El Ferrol was a city condemned to starvation.

About 1847, when the Marquis of Molíns assumed charge of the Ministry of the Navy, El Ferrol came to life again from its ashes, and the cycle of its misfortunes was ended. Its drydocks were repaired. New shipyards, light-houses, and moles were constructed, and the structures of the Navy Yard were rebuilt. The first steam-engine factory in the history of the Spanish Navy was built; and its com-plement, new shipyards. Once again El Ferrol was the scene of launching celebrations, events that had persisted only in the memory of its oldest inhabitants. In 1853 the *Rey Francisco de Asís* (King Francis of Assisi) had been launched into the water. For fifty years there had been no such occurrence. The city felt the beneficent influence of its straining shipyards, and was happy. It kept on giving its sons to the navy, and in its homes there was always the assurance that no vocation inspired by the sea should come to naught.

At this time there was living in El Ferrol a certain Francisco Franco Vietti, a son of mariners, a grandson and great-grandson of mariners, and the father of sons in whom was to be seen that same inclination to follow the career that opened from their very doorsteps. A sailor, too, was his father-in-law, Ladislao Baamonde[1] y Ortega, superintendent-general of the navy, as were his ancestors.

Franco Vietti was a man of medium stature, of vivacious intellect, and possessed of a frown that lent an air of severity and energy to his glance. His thick gray beard and bushy mustache emphasized his martial mien, very much in the fashion of the epoch. Methodical, austere, and pious, at fifty he was superintendent-general of the navy and the author of several textbooks. His schedule of living was changeless. Early on Saturday afternoon he went to the church of San Julián, where he prepared himself for his Sunday communion, which he would not dispense with for anything. At nightfall he retired to his home, where he gathered about him the members of his family and any guests who might be present to say the Rosary.

Franco Vietti was one of the children of Nicolás Franco y Sánchez, reviewing officer of the Administrative Body of the Navy, who married thrice and was the father of fifteen children. Shortly after reaching his twentieth year Franco Vietti married Hermenegilda Salgado Araujo y Pérez, of a family of El Ferrol, who was ten years older than her husband. She was small, home-loving, and possessed of a plenitude of spirit so needed then, when one realizes the vicissitudes of the era.

Seven sons were born of this marriage. The oldest, Nicolás, followed in the footsteps of his forebears. He entered the navy, and as paymaster on a warship he made two voyages to the Philippines. In 1890 he married the daughter of a landed family of El Ferrol named Pilar Baamonde y Pardo, daughter of Ladislao Baamonde, a commandant of the navy.

Pilar Baamonde had that delicate, transparent beauty that is the pride, almost the inheritance, of Galician women. An oval, symmetrical face, and pensive, melancholy eyes. When

---

[1] The name Baamonde is derived from the village of the same name in the province of Lugo, in northern Spain.

she reached maturity, Pilar was still very conservative in dress, in all that this connotes of nobility and respect, for this concept of dignity and modesty in dress did not in the least subtract from the admirable elegance of her bearing. A mistress always of herself, her moral courage strengthened by the intensive life of her spirit, she faced life's problems with a serenity and a fortitude that might be called stoical were they not more aptly described as Christian.

Five children were born of this marriage: Nicolás, the oldest, and Paquito (Francisco), Pilar, Ramón, and Pazita. The youths, heeding the call of the army, left their home at a very early age to enroll in military academies. All except Pazita who died at the age of five.

Far away though they were from El Ferrol, the glory of her sons did not fail to reach that white-walled cottage with its green blinds; Francisco, the youngest general in the army, commander-in-chief of the Legion, a general at thirty-two; Ramón, the hero of the ship *Plus Ultra*, who traced in his flight triumphal arches over the sea and Spanish America.

Their mother smiled, happy, and hid herself from the eyes of the curious. In vain the people sought her to give her the congratulations they wished to tender to her absent sons. She was to be seen neither in the streets nor at receptions. But she did not fail to attend for a single night the classes which she taught in the Workers' Night School, and there was nothing that could make her break this apostolate of duty she had chosen for herself.

When Ramón, flying out into the darkness of the Atlantic, stirred the world, the mother of the flyer was calm. And when on another flight Ramón was lost in the sea, and the days passed, without a sign, the lady showed herself unruffled and resigned, and those who went to console her left rebuffed, for the mother of the heroes had that same sublime courage which she had passed on to her sons.

She was neither dismayed in days of trial and tribulation nor vain in hours of triumph. The arrival of Ramón at

Pernambuco was celebrated in El Ferrol with a *Te Deum,* from which Pilar Baamonde was not missing. The public was waiting afterwards at the door to applaud her, but she did not appear. Upon inquiry, the curious discovered that she had left through another entrance.

All this did not indicate an utter scorn of human glory, but rather a singular tendency of the spirit to flee from all that might seem vain and frivolous. "The laurels," she used to say, "are for my sons, who deserve them." She was satisfied to give thanks to heaven during long hours of prayer which she spent in the solitude of the churches of El Ferrol.

On February 28, 1934, while traveling through Madrid, Pilar Baamonde Pardo passed away. She was sixty-eight years of age. Death took her when she was preparing to make a pilgrimage to Rome.

The register of the military parish of San Francisco, El Ferrol, records the note that on the 17th of December, 1892, was celebrated the baptism of Francisco Franco Baamonde, "who was born one half hour after midnight on the 4th day of that month, and who was baptized with the names of Francisco, Paulino, Hermenegildo, and Teódulo; the son of the naval paymaster Nicolás Franco and Pilar Baamonde."

There was a school in El Ferrol named The School of the Sacred Heart. It was founded by Marcos Vázquez, a priest of exemplary habits, and following his death the good work was carried on by Manuel Comellas, an upright man, jealously and paternally solicitous of the welfare of the children entrusted to his care. Francisco Franco received his early education in this school, and, following a course then traditional in El Ferrol, he entered the Naval School, which was directed by the war-sloop captain, Saturnino Suances, where he pursued the studies leading to the bachelor's degree and other subjects required for entrance to the Naval Academy.

It happened, however, that at that time the Spanish Treasury was laboring under difficult circumstances, and extensive economies had to be resorted to in order to balance accounts. One of the economies consisted in the reduction of the personnel of the army and navy, and a suspension until further notice of the entrance examinations of the Naval Academy. Francisco Franco was one of those affected by this measure. He adjusted his situation, however, by taking the entrance examinations of the Toledo Military Academy, which he entered on August 29, 1907, and from which he was graduated on the 13th of July, 1910, with the rank of second lieutenant.

Franco was a slender youth, of delicate features and large, shining, curious eyes. He was very devoted and always ready to discharge the duties, no matter how rigorous, which the discipline of the Academy imposed. At the same time he was restless, and of a merry, lively disposition that led him to take part in all of the pranks and adventures that were a part of those colorful years as a cadet.

As a second lieutenant he served the first period of his military career in the Zamora Regiment No. 8, stationed at El Ferrol. But Franco's youth rebelled against the immobility of life in the garrison at El Ferrol. It seems that in the innermost recesses of his soul there struggled that verse of Shelley, that Lyautey accepted as his slogan: "The soul's joy lies in doing."

And up from Morocco there grumbled a warlike roar that shattered like thunder over Spain. Franco listened attentively. For an officer of his age, such a curiosity for Africa in those times was strange and unusual.[2]

---

[2] For centuries Spain has held cities and territory in Morocco on the northern coast of Africa (Ceuta, Melilla, Peñón de la Gomera, Alhucemas, etc.). She has been concerned about the future of these possessions — which were in complete decadence at the close of the nineteenth century — because of their strategic importance in relation to Spanish trade, and their close proximity to the coast of Andalusia. Except for the so-called "African War" of 1859, there were never any expansionist desires either on the part of the people or government of Spain in Morocco in the nineteenth century. However, French activities in Morocco, and the internal anarchy which existed there, both of which endangered the security of Spanish trade in the Mediterranean, caused Spain to become increasingly concerned about African affairs. It was a strategic relationship similar to England's interest in Gibraltar.

In the partitioning of Africa prior to the World War Spain kept close watch. A treaty was signed with France in 1904 whereby Spain was given control over a zone in northern Morocco, and the international Algeciras Conference in 1906, following the brusque intervention of Germany in Moroccan affairs, entrusted to Spain and France the policing of the region. Shortly after this there began a series of native uprisings in both the French and Spanish zones which were very costly to Spain. A new treaty with France in 1912 established a Spanish "zone of influence" in northern Morocco. But Spanish control there was destined to be a tragic story of continuous war waged against native tribes which refused to be incorporated into the patterns of Spanish society. Morocco became Spain's burden. (Note by Translator.)

CHAPTER II

Franco in Melilla

THE year 1911 was begun under the sign of Morocco. The echoes of the recent parliamentary debates over the campaign of 1909 — the battle of Sidi Musa, the Ravine of the Lobo — still resounded, and as a result of this debating the people of Spain had aligned themselves into two opposing camps. While one group demanded that Spain withdraw from Morocco, the other asked for a complete conquest of the Riffs.

But suddenly an event of transcendental importance was announced: the voyage of the King to Melilla to visit the conquered territory. On the 5th of January, Alfonso XIII left Spain accompanied by the Prime Minister, Canalejas, and a magnificent retinue. A great reception was tendered him in Melilla. The King inspected the positions, and the trip inspired an outburst of writing, ardent with praise and embellished with the highest hopes. There were some who exhumed the last will of Queen Isabella the Catholic. The statement that Spain's future lay in Africa was repeated, and some newspapers even demanded that the King be given the title "Africanus." Canalejas himself, reflecting on his impressions of the trip, said, "Today is opened a new era for our aggrandizement, and a new chapter in the history of Spain."

With that versatility that characterizes the Spanish people, forgetful and optimistic by nature, they began to count their chickens before they were hatched. They promised for the recently conquered lands, dry and barren though they were, things that they denied to the fertile fields of the Peninsula. There was talk of building bridges on the African coast, of exploiting mines, of opening up natural resources, which existed in most cases only in the imaginations of the dreamers. One needs only to remember what Spain controlled, and the precarious conditions under which she exercised that control. Finally, the dark background of the year 1909 faded into the distant horizon.

Toward the middle of the same year, 1911, some ships of the Spanish squadron stationed off the coast of Larache landed several companies of soldiers, who occupied this city and Alcazarquivir with the purpose of protecting the nationals residing there. The enemies of what was called "the Moroccan adventure" were angered and excited, especially the liberal ex-Minister Miguel Villanueva, who distinguished himself for his tenacious opposition. Not only in Spain did these disembarkments provoke polemics and uneasiness, but also abroad. The Moroccan question was the burning issue of the day that worried all the chancelleries of Europe. France, which had landed troops at Casablanca, ordered them up to Fez. England spoke of her rights in Tangier. And on the first of July a German gunboat, the *Panther,* was seen anchored off Agadir, landing troops to protect German subjects in accordance with the established formula used in order to justify the occupation of African territory.

Spain was engaged in this diplomatic struggle when on the 24th of August an official *communique* reported that the topographical commission of the General Staff, under the leadership of Major Molina Cádiz, and escorted by two companies of troops, had been attacked in the neighborhood of the River Kert, being forced to fall back with five casualties.

The Captain-General of Melilla, Aldave, following the example of General Marina in 1909, decided to undertake a punitive expedition immediately. On the 31st of August a column of five thousand men under the command of General Larrea left to occupy the Talusits, small heights overlooking the river. And on the same day that the government in Madrid was publishing an explanatory note on the incident in the River Kert region, "congratulating itself that the Riffian incident could be considered closed," a new war was begun.

The spectacle of the departure of troops for Morocco was repeated, with demonstrations pro and con on the sidewalks. A new reluctance filled those who could see no end to this adventure. The journalistic wrangling was deafening. Parliamentary debates and notices of ministerial crises were in order. And all the time more soldiers marched forth, and the sick and the wounded returned, who described the region occupied as a land of terror under a blazing sun that, with the aid of mosquitoes and brackish waters, broke down the healthiest constitution with fever and organic disorders, when one was lucky enough to escape attacks and return unwounded from the front lines.

"The troops," wrote General Serra Orts, who directed that campaign, "were in a constant stalemate; denied sleep, eating little and poorly, as their critical and dangerous position required. During those eleven interminable hours in the defense of the Talusits, no one ate, drank, or rested for a single moment. They slept, when it was possible to sleep, in the open air. Sixty-five per cent of the men, of all ranks, from generals to privates, were the victims of malaria."

The year ended without any abatement in the fighting begun in August. General Ordóñez and three colonels were in the list of the dead.

If life was disagreeable and difficult for the advance guard, it was little worse than that in Melilla, where attacks became so frequent that the Military Command prohibited entry or departure from the city after sunset. Furthermore, it suffered so from overcrowding — there were some forty-four thousand soldiers in the zone — that it was jammed to overflowing to the last hut, and it was necessary to use newly built stores and a native hospital as barracks.

During the first months of 1912 the intensity of the fighting abated. Spain was sick of hearing about Morocco. People were asking each other: "Will the war become a chronic affliction?" The bleeding memories of the year 1909 were recalled once more, and were all the more painful in a country wasted by the loss of its colonies. The newspapers that manipulated public opinion sharpened their hostility toward the war and the generals. The incidents of each day were gathered in a section which invariably bore the heading: "The Tragedy of Morocco." Revolutionary propaganda utilized the campaign for its destructive activity. "Not another man nor peseta for a war that only defends the interests of the mining companies. Let us quit Morocco!"

This depression reached the army. The majority of the soldiers considered it the worst punishment possible to have it their lot to serve in Africa. Many of the officers looked forward with horror to their years of sojourn in that inhospitable land, which their regulations prescribed.

One morning in February of the year 1912, a small, slender lieutenant disembarked at Melilla. He was almost a boy; a good drawing-room officer. Melilla was then a dirty, tumble-down city, that had to improvise space for the great agglomerations that the struggle was allotting to it. There was a scarcity of many materials. Uncomfortable, disheveled, the city was in that penumbra that forms the transition from barbarism to civilization. It was populated by a heterogeneous assortment of people, among whom drifted that legion of ragged adventurers that gather like flies at the smell of war: bootblacks, valise sellers, vendors of fried fish, almonds, and candy. The sun, beating on the white-washed walls, and drawing resplendent sparkles from the sea, dazzled the young officer with its brilliance. It was the light of a new continent. Africa!

From the wharf he went to the barracks occupied by the African Regiment No. 68. He had arrived to fill the post which he had requested voluntarily. That officer was Francisco Franco.

At that time, with the purpose of lightening the bloody tribute which Morocco claimed with such cruel stubbornness from the Peninsula, Dámaso Berenguer was organizing the native police force which later came to be called "Regulars," formed entirely of Moors, that were to fight in their own way under the command of Spanish officers. This force was intended to form the vanguard as shock troops, bearing the heaviest brunt of the fighting. Volunteers were sought to make up the officers. Volunteers for glory and for death. Among the first to enroll was to be seen the name of Franco. The adventure of war attracted the youth with an irresistible seduction.

CHAPTER III

The Call to Arms

DURING the first months of 1912 the struggle languished on the banks of the River Kert, which is a bed of gravel during most of the year. The columns commanded by Generals Larrea, Zubía, Carrasco, Villalón, and Pereira spent their time in exploration and reconnaissance, without any serious mishaps. They suffered nocturnal attacks, already of customary occurrence, and sniping, which was as common in the Riff country as if it were a product of the climate.

But it was impossible to guarantee even a moderate measure of security while El Mizzian, a dervish who was stirring up war with his preaching and who scoured over the basin of the Kert at the head of his fanatics, exciting them to fight ceaselessly, was allowed his life and liberty. El Mizzian was the mosquito that spread the virus of war.

Through painful efforts that cost them much blood, they succeeded in dominating the river, fortifying it as a boundary, and the troops of General Aldava advanced over the plains of El Garet. Monte Arruit and Tumiat were occupied.

As we have already indicated, Dámaso Berenguer, after staying a few months in Algeria, where he studied the organization of native troops, introduced troops of the same kind in the Spanish zone. They were called "Native Regulars of Melilla." How cautiously they were regarded at first! "These men," said the more suspicious, "will pass over to the enemy with arms as soon as they are given the opportunity." The officers themselves did not feel very certain of them, so many tales were current about what had happened to the

French with similar troops. The forces were organized first in Sidi Guariach, whence they were transferred to an encampment in the neighborhood of Monte Arruit.

On the 12th of May they received the order to leave for Zeluán; and when they arrived they were obliged to pass the night outside the fortified Alcazaba. Suspicion was increasing. The Native Regulars — for the most part Algerians — were considered armed enemies in one's own backyard. Spies declared that insubordination was fermenting among the three companies and the three squads that made up the force. At the head of the troops went Berenguer. The cavalry was commanded by Major Miguel Cabanellas, and Francisco Franco was a second lieutenant in one of the companies. That night the officers decided to maintain a special guard in order to avoid any disagreeable surprise.

On the 14th of May the Regulars left for Yadumen to take part in one of the operations. A company in which Franco was serving with his section, and the third squad commanded by Emilio Fernández Pérez, the sections of which were led by the First Lieutenants Samaniego, Llarch, Núñez de Prado, and Ibáñez de Aldecoa, was ordered to spread out. The enemy opened fire as soon as they saw the deployment of the Spanish troops. The company of infantry had as its objective the conquest of the town of Haddú-Allal-u-Kaddur. It was meeting a tenacious resistance, which the Regulars were beating back, raising up and forcing out the enemy, who lay flattened out on the ground.

From a hill Colonel Berenguer was following with binoculars the progress of the troops. The body of light horsemen that went in the vanguard to the right attracted his attention particularly. "That section is advancing very well," he observed.

"That section is led by Franco," answered another.

On that day Franco received his baptism of fire.

The company kept on going forward, and it was already on the outskirts of the town when a throng of Moors appeared, with great pomp and ostentation, led by a solemn, bearded man with a billowing white cape, a magnificent horseman on a steed that caracoled about nervously. He came on haughtily, gesticulating, crying out in loud and pompous tones. The others followed him with blind confidence. The sudden appearance of this army was endangering the Regulars, when the sure fire of a corporal by the name of Gonzalo Sauca brought the majestic Moor to the ground. An instantaneous change was produced in the multitude. The Moorish horsemen, who a moment before had been so determined and headlong, remained paralyzed, as if some mysterious power had suddenly held them back. They wavered for a few moments, but only to break out immediately in flight, terrified, making gestures of intense grief and panic.

That majestic Moor was El Mizzian, the same one who had proclaimed a hundred times that only a golden bullet could kill him. With the death of El Mizzian his army disintegrated, and the campaign decayed. In the months following the troops advanced without meeting any resistance, and they consolidated their control over El Garet, an immense expanse of three hundred and sixty square miles.

The tempest of war was followed by a calm. Spain and her troops well needed it. The nation, which felt an aversion toward the conflict, breathed easily when it was told that there was to be no more fighting. The native troops were sent to the encampment of Sebt, where they were to remain for thirteen months.

But the war that had been snuffed out in Melilla was to flare up again in the western zone. On the 18th of February, 1913, General Alfau left Ceuta at the head of a column of two thousand five hundred men, and arrived at Tetuán without firing a single shot. They were received with demonstrations of sympathy on the part of the populace.

This city of the Moors, which once again became Spain's, awakened the interest of the curious. The novels of Alarcón were dusted off, and the names of O'Donnell and Prim were recalled. People spoke of the picturesque beauty of Tetuán, the enchantment of its various quarters, the clamor of its market places, the secret of its mosques, the labyrinth of its narrow streets, with their trade of brilliant textiles, embroidered slippers, perfumes and hammered metalware, damascene scimitars, amber and sandalwood, and the sensual effeminacy of its inhabitants, the chants of the muezzin, calling the people to prayer, its courtyards of blue and of red ocher, and its mournful music. Through the painful narratives of endless fighting and through the calcine, sandy vistas of Melilla, the city of Tetuán was a jewel which Africa offered as a compensation and a gift for the sacrifices of Spain.

But the satisfaction brought by the event was of short duration. The multitudes that surrounded the city were not willing to allow the Spaniards to enjoy the fruits of their conquest in peace. They were restless. In the outskirts, attacks became more frequent, and Tetuán was forced to enclose itself in a corset of breastworks. In order to relieve the city of that burden, Laucien, a city six miles distant, was occupied, but the situation was unchanged. Every convoy which was sent to the new position meant a battle.

In June of 1914 matters became worse, and the Regulars were obliged to depart hurriedly to the western zone. They went on foot from the encampment to Melilla in a hellish heat. Two soldiers died of sunstroke. They stopped at Ceuta, where they passed the night, and the following day, before reaching Tetuán, they were forced to deploy for a skirmish and open fire, because the enemy was attacking the positions of Río Martín, which were asking urgently for help.

Soon the rebellion in the neighborhood of Tetuán extended to the road leading to Ceuta and had spread to the zone of Larache. The Raisuni, the lord of Beni-Arós, was preaching a holy war and was stirring up the tribes.

Franco was right in the middle of this hornets' nest, in

command of his section of Regulars. In September the great battle of Izardúy took place, where, in the opinion of Dámaso Berenguer, Franco's military temperament was revealed, in conquering, with a skill that was a credit to his vocation as a soldier, and with a vigor that was a reflection of his valor, some heights which the enemy were defending with a terrific determination. Franco earned his first promotion by merits in war through this action. He was now a first lieutenant.

And the months of wearisome, overwhelming war went on, without any definite result. Sometimes treaties were made with the Raisuni, but the occupation of territory, and attacks did not cease. At other times relations were broken off completely, and open warfare was resumed.

The year 1915 was one of constant guerrilla fighting, consisting of skirmishing at the water holes, relieving the positions, protecting the roads, and opening them when they were closed by the incursions of the Moors.

In this dull, daily, chronic struggle, encamping among cliffs, fighting with ice and snow and devilish heat, the spirit of that slender, delicate-appearing officer was tempered, and his warrior's soul was forged. He was always courageous and ever ready to perform the duties entrusted to him, no matter how difficult and arduous they might be; gambling with his life every day, with a graceful indifference. The High Command appreciated his work, and recommended him for a promotion by merits in the field. Franco was a captain soon after reaching his twentieth birthday.

At the end of the year 1915, of the forty-two generals and officers of the Native Regulars of Melilla, all volunteers, only seven remained unwounded. Among them was Franco. He seemed as if invested with mythical powers that made him invulnerable. He might have boasted that the bullet had not yet been made which was to kill him. Soldiers and officers fell in great numbers in the fighting. Franco always came back smiling and unscathed. One day while on a parapet he picked up a thermos bottle to drink some coffee. A bullet fired with diabolical accuracy tore the cork from between his fingers. The Captain did not change countenance; he drank the contents, and turning toward the enemy camp, he cried: "Better luck next time!"

But in the year 1916 his lucky star was to suffer an eclipse. On the 29th of June, an agreement having been made with the Raisuni, the troops from Ceuta and Larache performed certain operations in the region of the Anghera tribe. The troops from Larache took Tafugallz, Melusa, and Ain Guenine, but the troops from Ceuta, in occupying Buit, had to undergo a very severe battle. The enemy were repulsed several times only to rally and renew the attack with the intention of overwhelming the Spanish lines. Francisco Franco was serving in the force from Ceuta. As he perceived that the enemy were harassing and impeding the advance from a parapet, he put himself at the head of his troops to take it by storm. He recalls that at that moment he picked up from the ground a rifle abandoned by a wounded Regular and loaded it to fire.

He took a few steps and fell to the ground with a bullet through his abdomen. "I felt," he was to say years later, "as if I had been clapped with a fiery plaster that was burning me up, cutting short my breath."

The wound was very critical, and Franco stayed in the advance position, because the physicians forbade that he be carried away to a hospital, fearful that he would die on the wayside. His parents arrived at Buit with the apprehension that they would not find their son alive. But their son lived, improved, and was soon convalescent. "The wound," declared the physician, "has followed a miraculous course." He recovered, and he was transferred to the Peninsula for his convalescence.

The merits which he had won during the last three years of constant service served to recommend him for a promotion, which was not granted, because in those days there were officers in certain positions who were markedly antagonistic to this sort of reward. The policy of restraining promotions through merits in war was the rule. The true motive, on the other hand, for such opposition to the recommendation, a motive which was only whispered in confidential tones and in specific army centers, was another. Franco was too young to be a high commanding officer in the army. He was only twenty-three years old!

Too young! A fortunate handicap which did not prevent him from behaving during those unlucky years as a veteran well endowed with experience, and which his superiors did not consider in entrusting to him missions and duties of the highest importance. And above all, there was his record. A man in full youth, covered with laurels, was to some immobile minds which graded promotions through years of military service, an anachronism.

The promotion was not granted to Franco; but on the other hand, he was compensated with the Cross of María Cristina.

The Captain resorted to the measures prescribed by the regulations in order to defend his rights, and he pressed a petition to the King in solicitation of a better compensation. The merits which he alleged, were of such a quality and so numerous that to ignore them would have amounted to an abandonment of justice, denying it to one of the best soldiers of Spain. The petition was satisfactorily adjusted. Franco ascended to the rank of Major, and as soon as he recuperated his military aptitudes, he asked again for a command of troops in Africa. But due to the lack of a vacancy, he had to accept an obligatory appointment in the Peninsula. He was assigned to the Prince's Regiment, garrisoned in Oviedo.

At that time there happened to be coincidentally in the capital of Asturias several officers whose names, as time went on, were to stand out prominently in the annals of the army: Alvaro Sueiro, Camilo Alonso Vega, Francisco Franco Salgado, at the present time aide to the Generalissimo,

Rafael Civantos, Valcázar, and Pardo — all these were, in the journey of life, to meet again their commanding officer for the accomplishment of memorable deeds.

The Asturian folk, so familiarized with the affectionate, diminutive youth, dubbed Franco "the little major." Invariably in the early part of the afternoon Franco would emerge from the hotel located on Uría Street, where he lodged, and mount his horse for his customary ride. The people would gather around to look at him. "The little major! So serious, so proud, and so young!" they would say. "He's just a boy!" He was the youngest major in the Spanish army. When he would enter the dining hall of the hotel, a wave of admiration would sweep through the room. The lodgers whispered to one another: "Franco."

How was I to know, a student then, that there were to come these days, in which the man eating at the next table was to relate to me such a moving and extensive story?

But Franco had not passed through Africa and through the war with impunity. He was never to forget them. It is the tormenting homesickness suffered by all the colonials who have given up their hearts to that exotic land. Franco had engraved on his retina scenes that would never erase themselves. His soul was conditioned and propitious to a restlessness that Spain would not satisfy. On his memory there weighed constantly the remembrance of those who were left behind, on the plains of El Garet, in the mountains of Tetuán, battling the Moor, living the uncertain hours of the campaign. The call of Africa echoed in his soul, first timidly and insinuative, and then as the fascination of a mirage, ensnaring him within its deadly grip. Africa!

Lethargic plains, under a blazing sun, roads through ravines, desolation, verdure of the gardens of Tetuán, the white balconies of Ceuta over the Straits of Gibraltar, pulse of the world. And far beyond all this, the mystery. The mystery of the sacred forests of Beni-Arós, the impenetrable secret of Xauen, the unknown lands of Axdir, roads that had never felt the tread of Europeans and nights with bonfires on the mountaintops, calling to war.

Franco already had in his veins the poison of Africa, the magic that had bewitched so many mortals who peered at the continent as curious ones or came to it as merchants or as warriors, remaining captives there forever. The unfathomable mystery of Africa, that watches over its secrets; with its clear, transparent nights, its suffocating, scorching days, its languid, sighing cadences, and the flaming passion in its burning, spying eyes. Major Franco had on file permanently a petition to return to Africa; and to Africa he returned.

CHAPTER IV

Franco in the Foreign Legion

ON THE 28th of April, 1920, the government in Madrid created the "Foreign Legion," entrusting to Lieutenant-Colonel José Millán Astray the task of its organization. No one seemed more endowed with such exceptional and appropriate aptitudes to carry out such a task; impetuous, fearless, possessing a clear understanding of military training, he had in full those qualities required for the leadership of a force that was to be the bravest of the brave.

Millán Astray devoted himself entirely to his labor. Years afterwards he was to relate the beginnings of this institution: "When I was charged with organizing the Legion, I thought first about the type of men that my Legionnaires were to be; and they were to be what they are today. After that, I pondered on those who would be the commanders who were to aid me in this enterprise, and I picked out Franco first of all. I telegraphed him offering him a post as my lieutenant. He accepted immediately, and here we were working together to organize the Legion. I chose the officers in the same manner, and soon Arredondo, the first captain, Olavide, the first lieutenant, and all the rest arrived."

In October of 1920 Franco found himself in Algeciras with the first ones who had joined the Legion. They were adventurers from all parts of the globe, dressed in odd and careless fashion; a collection of Bohemian types thrown together only in the great emotion of war. He crossed the straits of Gibraltar with them. He contemplated them with sympathy, for he knew that they were all to perform the same deeds together.

Soon after landing in Ceuta, they passed haughtily in review before the lieutenant-colonel, as he harangued them. Franco felt the emotion then beclouding his eyes. "It is," he says, "the dawning of the Legionnaire's feeling."

Who were these men, that so affected the Major, and toward whom extended his feeling of admiration? The majority of them hid their true names, and some even their origin. They were adventurous foreigners, Spaniards wandering over uncertain roads that had no end, discharged civil guards, former soldiers; all with true military backbone, persons with a scorn of danger and men who flirted with death — a former officer of the Prussian Guard, an Italian aviator, a secularized monk who desired to return to his monastery, but upon whom his prior had imposed a strange penance: enlistment in the Foreign Legion.

On October 16, the three newly formed companies of the First Banner (Primera Bandera) installed themselves in the encampment of Riffian. Forty Legionnaires left, in the first sortie of the Legion, in the capacity of muleteers for the operations at Xauen. The rest watched them leave with envy.

On November 2 the Banner commanded by Franco left for Uad Lau, and at nightfall it reached the town of Rincón. The second stage of the journey ended in Tetuán. The vanguard uttered cries of joy when they discerned the silhouettes of the minarets outlining themselves in the distant blue. The Legionnaires marched through the Plaza of Spain before the curious gaze of the people, who saw for the first time that force which, without having yet fought an engagement, was already surrounded by an aureola of bravery. They bivouacked on the hills of Beni-Madan. As their muleteers had lost their way and did not arrive, a hasty meal was improvised, and the Legionnaires slept uncovered on the ground or on the canvas of their cots.

The third and last day of the march, very difficult on account of the rain, ended in the pleasant valley of the Lau, surrounded by tropical jungle and in full view of the sea. The imposing outline of the mountains of Gomara shut off the horizon to one side. On the other, the range of Beni-Hassan, with its mantles of snow, was the citadel protecting the treasure of Xauen. The terrain was sloping, and a mile and a half away could be seen the seashore with its rolling waves.

Here, in Uad Lau, the camp was established; the first encampment of the Legion, and in it, as Franco said, the Legionnaires of the First Banner were to prepare for war. An iron discipline was imposed upon them; they were trained for combat and given target practice. Night duties were carried out scrupulously. No one slept. The officer maintained a constant vigil outside his tent, inspecting the positions and discharging his various duties. "This is the active and vigorous life of the officers of the Legion."

At night the officers met, presided over by Franco, and discussed the problems of the Moroccan war and the adaptation of the rules and regulations to it.

In Uad Lau there were no distractions other than those that the camp naturally offered. The arrival of mail was a joy, and the appearance of the gunboat *Bonifaz* was a memorable event. The navy officer Juan Cervera, who was in command, and the other officers landed and spent an afternoon with the Legionnaires. How this visit was appreciated by everyone!

Christmas Eve of the year 1920 was celebrated in Uad Lau in the best manner possible. There was a splendid feast, music, and great merriment. The German Legionnaires set up a Christmas tree on the branches of which the officers hung as gifts some bottles of beer.

It appeared as if the hour would never come when they would leave Uad Lau. That solitude and that monotony wearied them. "We are," wrote Franco, "weary of the peace in which we live. The Banner is perfectly trained and in hopes of being used. The Legionnaires dream of going to

Xauen, mounting the valley of the Lau, and joining the coast with the mysterious city. Our wait seems endless."

But one day in April, the 17th, Colonel Castro Girona arrived at the camp, and soon after, Millán Astray, who was at the head of a column composed of the Tabors of Tetuán and Ceuta, of the Mejala Xerifiana, and forces of light infantry and artillery.

Who would have recognized Uad Lau, filled with that uproar and that animation? Scenes of joy accompanied the meeting of fellow officers again. Spirals of smoke, the music of popular songs rose from the camp. No one slept that night.

The colonel called together all the commanding officers and explained to them the projected operation: the occupation of Kaaseres, the key point of Targa and Tiguisats, in order to make more secure the occupation of the coast of Gomara and avoid as far as possible the dangers that might arise through the action of several tribes which the Raisuni was trying to provoke to rebellion.

At dawn on the 18th the column waded across the Lau and reached the corner of Kaaseres. Warships aided in the operation. As the advance continued, the valley of the Targa was sighted in all its spring luxuriance, an idyllic landscape, with its green, flowery gardens, and its cottages of shining white. In the afternoon, the High Command, Dámaso Berenguer, arrived.

On the following day the column traversed broad fields adorned with olive groves and blooming orange trees, finally reaching the valley of Tiguisats. In the immediate vicinity of the mouth of the river of the same name, the troops camped. There the Legion remained four days, at the end of which it returned to Uad Lau.

Soon after, on the 30th of April, the First Banner was incorporated with the column of Castro Girona, which was to open up the communication of Xauen with the seacoast, and establish a definitive line or military frontier, forming communication between the Atlantic and the Mediterranean, which by route of Larache-Alcázar-Lucus-Xauen-Uad Lau would be a regular highway around the great bulk of Xebala, thus isolating Nuhaxen and Yebel-Alam, the eagle's nest of its crests and the refuge of Edrisi's fanaticism.

The route took them through a chaos of mountains, through defiles, along yawning chasms and devilish paths from which the mules slipped headlong with a clatter. An asphyxiating heat made progress all the more painful. Blockhouses were left scattered at points all along the road.

The troops stopped at every brook to quench their thirst, which was devouring them with the fieriness of fever. They halted at Tagsut. The next day, early in the morning, they pressed on toward the mountains of Kálaa, and in the afternoon, illuminated with the glow of twilight, the longed-for vision of Xauen arose, with its haughty fortress, red-tiled roofs, and exuberant foliage. Xauen, which but a few months before the Spanish forces had incorporated into civilization, arousing it from its age-old lethargy.

In the holy city the three Banners joined together for the first time. The London *Times,* referring to these operations, said: "After a painful march through a difficult terrain, the Spanish columns have established communication between Xauen, the sacred city occupied last autumn, and the Mediterranean. The success of the operations, in which the newly created body, the Legion, took part, is owed in large part to the opportune political actions which preceded them."

On the 4th of May, the Legionnaires under the command of Franco were serving in the column of Sanjurjo. "We are downcast," said the Major, "because we are not in the vanguard." The enemy made known their presence and the Legionnaires answered the first shots with cries of "Long live Spain!" and "Long live the Legion!" Two fell wounded.

On the following day the Banner stationed themselves in

the shadow of the blockhouse of Miskrela. With honest envy the Legionnaires watched the guerrillas of the Regular advance. At the end of the operations the city was left free of enemy pressure. The First and Third Banners were left as a garrison in Xauen.

The days spent there were a constant school of war. On May 24 the First Banner left to take part in the campaign of Beni-Arós, which was to put an end to the Raisuni, nerve of all the rebellion in the western zone. Franco and his Legionnaires arrived at Zoco del Arbaa, and in conjunction with the column of Sanjurjo, took part in the operations of Beni-Lait.

"Our hope of alternating in the vanguard," wrote Franco, "is being disillusioned, and the officers march sadly and pensively. We have trained our soldiers to serve in the most dangerous posts, and for this also were gathered under these Banners a group of enthusiastic and determined officers. The soldiers seem to share in our disappointment, and they mount in silence the slopes of Beni-Lait, up to now the hiding place of enemy snipers."

And Franco's lamentation because they were kept from the honor of being in the vanguard continued. "This is too much. We did not come to Morocco a second time for this," muttered one officer. "No one is satisfied. Great chagrin can be noted on the countenance of our commanding officer. He counsels moderation. The day will come. But deep in our hearts we are all discouraged. What will become of our creed?"

Disillusion was changed to disconsolateness. The Legionnaire, upon seeing himself held back from the post of danger, considered himself disqualified, diminished in his qualities, punished in his prestige. He demanded the vanguard, not as an honor alone, but also as a right. Franco summed up the feelings of his companions when he complained thus: "If the Legion," he thought, "is not to be more courageous than all the rest of the forces, and its bravery an example, why did these men join the Legion?" And he could find no answer.

One afternoon the Legionnaires were granted a more advanced position, but the Major was bound previously to allow no casualties.

After a day of rest, the Legion left with the column for the operation at Salah. "Our place," Franco insisted, "has not changed. As the days go on, our vexation increases, and we are respectfully begging the General to give us a post of honor, to let us serve some day in the vanguard."

Five days later the most important combat of the cycle of operations at Beni-Arós was in progress. The fighting lasted throughout the entire day. One unit was without rest for twenty-six hours between march and combat. A rally of the enemy compelled the intervention of the Legionnaires, who paid for that inaugural deed with the coin current in war; at the price of their heroic blood. Various soldiers fell wounded, and the Captain of the First Company, Pablo Arredondo — the "protomartyr" officer of the Legion — had his legs riddled through with bullets, but refused to be retired from his post. General Berenguer was to state in his memoirs: "The battle was a very stubborn one. To be especially noted are the great resistance and aggressiveness which the enemy offered, and the splendid behavior of the Foreign Legion, which was initiated on that day into its first formal battle."

Early in June, the First Banner was sent to the zone of Larache. Since the valley of Amegatet, from Timisar to Buharrax, was controlled, and the rebellion had extended almost to the very foot of the eastern slopes of the mountain, the space available for advance in this region being therefore exhausted, the moment had come to take action on the western slope, occupying the valley of Beni-Arós, once the obstacles opposing such action had been swept aside.

The march was made under a leaden sun, in a sticky, ennervating heat. On the 10th the Banner passed the night in the encampment of Rokba-el-Gozal, after taking part in the operations in the sierra of Sidi Embarek. In the succeeding days the Legionnaires went through the forests to Zoco del Jemis, arriving at Bab-es-Sor, "The Gateway of the Fortress," from the summit of which could be described in the distance the settlement of Tazarut, the haunt of the Raisuni. The operations had been developed with the precision of perfect maneuvers. Franco did not hide the pleasure produced in him by the sight of the cavalry from Larache as it ran through the mountains, like a flying column of centaurs.

The First Banner camped at Rokba-Gozal. It was already clear in the minds of all that the objective to be obtained which would conclude the campaign was the conquest of Tazarut. With it would break and crumble the power of the Raisuni. Tazarut was besieged by the columns during the next few days, and the soldiers had before their eyes constantly the sight of those little white huts, surrounded by forests.

There was no other topic of conversation at meals, which the officers ate in the open air on account of the suffocating heat. A gust of furnace heat, warmed in the forges of the Sahara, passed over the camp. From the surrounding fields there came a symphony of howls and cries, from all the fauna, exultant with the heat. An officer remarked: "Today the heat reached sixty degrees centigrade. Tomorrow . . ." and he looked at the cloudless sky, its myriad dazzling pinpoints. "Tomorrow we shall be in the gardens of Tazarut," answered another. There was no other thought or desire. To advance, to conquer new lands, to enter distant and mysterious cities, and raise over them the flag they loved, was the dream that urged them on.

CHAPTER V

Melilla, 1921

THE encampment at Rokba-el-Gozal was sleeping peacefully, enclosed by the shadows of the mountains of Beni-Arós. It was the 21st of July. The earth exhaled the warm vapor of tropical respiration. Under the tents were sleeping the thousands of men who made up the columns that went in search of the Raisuni to defeat him.

In contrast with that calm, in the hut of the General Staff headquarters there was to be seen that excitement and confusion often produced in private homes at the sudden illness of a member of the family. The telephone rang constantly. The small field station pulsed like the heart of a man with fever, as it gathered the anguish that came trembling from out of space, and answered with disconsolate messages. The High Commissary spoke with the generals, prepared some orders, answered the telephone. The faces of those in the room reflected the pallor of fright.

What had happened in some distant outpost that reverberated with such tragic uneasiness in the quiet, tranquil camp of Rokba-el-Gozal, under the warm mantle of the summer night? The hours, far from soothing and pacifying that startling surprise, increased it and sharpened it.

The High Commissary put an end to that situation and wrote the following dispatch, to be sent to the Commander-General at Melilla:

"I am aware of the march of events, expecting that everyone will think of the prestige and the honor of the nation above all in this critical moment."

Then, addressing his aides, he said: "We are leaving for Tetuán within one hour."

At two in the morning, Lieutenant-Colonel Millán Astray ordered that Major Franco be summoned urgently. But as the messenger was on the point of leaving, he corrected himself and said, "No, don't go. I'll go myself."

Franco was standing at the entrance to his tent. He was undoubtedly expecting that visit.

"Is something wrong? Do we have to go out?"

The commander of the Legion replied, "One Banner must leave as soon as possible for Fondak."

Since there were three banners in Rokba-el-Gozal, Franco asked which one had to leave.

"The one that is ready the soonest."

Franco transmitted the order to the other commanders and they chose by lot. It fell to the first, Franco's Banner.

An hour and a half later the Legionnaires began their march toward Fondak. It was a tramp through forests, on whose boughs there trembled the first light of a day beginning sultry, with a sun of lead. A halt was made in Al-Ihudi, where the soldiers took advantage of the occasion to bathe in the river and restore their energy, for there were many miles yet to go. The most optimistic calculated that they would not reach Fondak until well into the night.

At three in the afternoon the march was resumed. Three in the afternoon — July — Africa. And since the heat was so terrific, they had to rest frequently, for the troops were becoming exhausted. Night fell over the marching men, who were now advancing over bare mountains, through gloomy defiles. Fondak seemed lost in a hopeless infinity. The hours lengthened for the Legionnaires, for to the fatigue which was overcoming them must be added their struggle with the hurricane that shook them endlessly with its blasts. At last the vanguards shouted: "Fondak!" Their last strength was revived. There, in the distance, the lights of the position glowed in the night. A long difficult climb yet remained.

When the soldiers reached Fondak, at eleven in the evening, they were completely exhausted. They did not wait for their dinner, and lost no time in setting up their tents. They unslung their knapsacks and threw themselves into the trenches. And there they slept.

But they did not all rest. This grace could not be granted to Franco. Hardly had he arrived at Fondak, when he was told that they had inquired for him from Tetuán insistently all afternoon and all night. And another call came soon.

"What is the Legion doing?"

"It is resting after twenty hours of continuous march."

"It is absolutely necessary for it to be in Tetuán at dawn."

"That is a physical impossibility; the soldiers cannot go on."

As dawn came on the telephone rang again; the same beseeching question, as if from a dying man, one shipwrecked: "When are they leaving?"

"The first thing in the morning."

"No! No! They must leave immediately. Right away. We cannot wait any longer. Melilla is falling!"

What sort of catastrophe had occurred to motivate such words: "Melilla is falling!"

Franco ordered reveille sounded. It was three in the morning. The bugle blew, but not a soldier stirred. Exhaustion had petrified them, and they had to be shaken one by one to be awakened. Once more they were on the march. How serious were the events occurring, that they made the signals of distress so desperately urgent, as if from a man drowning? At a quarter of ten the Legionnaires were marching through the streets of Tetuán on the way to the station, where the train was awaiting them. On the very platform a friend approached Franco and said in consternation, "General Fernández Silvestre has committed suicide."

In Ceuta the Banner embarked on the *Ciudad de Cádiz*, on which there also went Sanjurjo, who gave him some vague information of the disaster.

And still one night and one morning more before seeing Melilla! The hours seemed endless, without any news to calm that restlessness that gnawed those on board with its ferocious teeth. There was no news, but the cry for assistance ringing in their ears since the departure from camp persisted during the entire length of the voyage. It was the High Commissary, who was already in Melilla, who was sending out the messages:

"Proceed at maximum speed. When will the boat arrive?"

They answered: "We are going at full speed, and we shall arrive at approximately two o'clock."

Since it was Sunday, Mass was said on deck. The faces of all were dark with apprehension, and their minds were concentrated fixedly on Melilla, convulsed with agonizing shudders.

It was the death rattle: "Hurry up."

For those who waited in the office of the Military Command the *Ciudad de Cádiz* was advancing with exasperating slowness. At eleven in the morning it was not even within sight of the port.

Franco went in search of the Captain and questioned him. "We are going at full speed," he said. "The boat cannot go faster."

At last the houses of the city showed white to the sun in the distance. Melilla! The waterfront seemed full of people. A section of carabineers and a body of musicians were on the pier. The Legionnaires waved greetings from the deck, cheered, and sang the "Madelon," the first music to break forth amid the panic which was strangling the city. A gasoline launch approached the ship with an aide of the High Commissary. Officers, avidly inquiring, surrounded him.

"Of the Office of the Commander General of Melilla,"

said the adjutant, "there is nothing left. The army is defeated. The city is defenseless, and the people have gone mad, seized with panic. We have no news of the column of Navarro. It is but necessary to raise the morale of the population, bringing to it the confidence it needs, and most of their fancies will disappear."

"Never did a more intense moment hold our hearts," wrote Franco. "To the painful emotion of tragedy was joined the impression of the emotion of the people, expressed with cheers and applause. Our hearts bled, but the Legionnaires sang, and hope was reborn in the hearts of the people. . . . Sorrow clouded our eyes, but we had to laugh and sing; songs broke forth, and through cries of 'Long live Spain!' the frenzied people applauded madly our entry."

There were harangues by Millán Astray, music, and parades of Legionnaires as well as of the bearded warriors of Beni-Arós, among tears, sobs, cheers, and applause. The city had recuperated, was once more itself after its collapse. This is how the Legion, without fighting, won its first victory, where it was unknown, with its mere presence. "On that day," declared General Berenguer, "the Legion and its commander lent a positive service to our control and to the nation."

"Then," says Franco, "we experienced the most profound emotions of our military life. Our hearts lamented the defeat. As the fugitives arrived, they related the sad moments of their retreat: the troops in headlong flight, the cowardice, the heroism, all the details of the painful tragedy. Silvestre, deserted; Morales, dead; soldiers that reached the city unarmed; Zeluán, holding out; Nador, also. This was the news brought by these men, in whose eyes terror had dilated the pupils, and who spoke with fright of headlong chase, of Moors pursuing, of Moorish women who put an end to the wounded, of the dreadfulness of the disaster. They arrived naked, half conscious, like poor madmen."

CHAPTER VI

Blockhouse and Convoys

A FEW hours after disembarking the First Banner left for the front lines, where resistance was being organized with the intention of barring the way to the avalanches of Moors that were descending from Gurugú with the intent to enter Melilla.

Thenceforth the Legionnaires were in the front lines, the longed-for posts, which they were not to abandon as long as the campaign lasted. Always in the vanguard, the Banner was to leave behind it, among the barren crags and plains, the slopes and the ravines, a trail of blood and a row of graves. Its officers and privates fell, the flower of the Legion, for death picks out its victims from the two. The First Banner! First in everything, by having received the grace of the Legion's heroism, by its presence in Melilla, by its triumphs and its dead. The battalions arriving from the Peninsula — La Corona, Borbón, and Extremadura — marched from the pier to occupy the outer line of forts, and the Regulars of Ceuta, under the command of the unforgettable González Tablas, who had landed only a few hours after the Legion, were sent to Zoco del Had in answer to the pressing appeal of Abd-el-Kader. The Legionnaires took up positions on the slopes of Taguel Manin and Ait-Aisa. One section occupied the fortlet of Sidi-Musa. The rest of the forces fortified themselves in Sidi-Hamed.

From this position could be seen in the distance the town of Nador, and the bands of Moors engaged in sacking and arson, and the caravans drawing away with their booty. On the roof of a house near the sea a heliograph flashed out whenever it could its sparkling winks, signals of distress. "Why don't you come to our rescue?" the heliograph seemed to say. "Are you going to let us die helplessly?"

The Legionnaires asked themselves the very same question. "Why don't we go to save them?" Each time the calls were more anguished. The Commander of the Legion finally made up his mind and asked Franco: "Why don't we send them a succor of food and medicine with some volunteers? Is there no one willing to take part in such a deed?"

Franco answered him without wavering, "There are many."

In order to prove it, he put the question to his soldiers, and not one of them shirked from that voluntary sacrifice, that practically amounted to death. And the Major remarked, "That is how we want our Legionnaires to be." The High Command did not consider the attempt opportune, for the same reasons for which it denied the Commander of the Legion permission to go to the rescue of the besieged post. The city could not be left unprotected.

August was the month of blockhouses and convoys. While the army was being organized in Melilla, it was necessary to guarantee the security of the city by a series of blockhouses placed at the points that were the most strategic, and accordingly the most hotly contested by the enemy. There existed blockhouses with a longer record of war than many ancient cities. Attempts to bring supplies to these blockhouses provoked each day's fighting. Once the position had been established, the enemy knew that the resources which it contained were meager, and that after a certain length of time it would have to be stocked again with supplies. Once the contingency was anticipated, the rest was up to the bands of Moors that gathered like flies at the smell of the convoy. And every convoy was a battle. To get the munitions and food supplies into the position was a triumph not always achieved. When the ferocity and the number of Moors prevented it, affliction for those besieged beyond hope of assistance was left in their hearts, and was sharpened by regret at their failure.

All the units of the Legion passed the test of the blockhouses. There was among the latter one called "Mezquita," situated on the slopes of Gurugú, and which was attacked furiously every night. On one occasion the Moors succeeded in destroying it. The soldiers called it "The Blockhouse of Death." On the 16th of September a message was sent from the redoubt declaring that the enemy were attacking ceaselessly, and had already wounded the commanding officer and the majority of the defenders. At that moment there occurred a deed which, by its extraordinary character, has since entered novels and appeared on the motion-picture screen, and which Major Franco relates in the following manner:

"Lieutenant Agulla, who commanded the forces of the Legion that were being attacked in the Atalayón, wanted to go to the rescue, but he was not allowed to do so because his men were needed for the defense of his position. So then he gathered his men and asked for volunteers to go with a corporal to reinforce the blockhouse during the night. They all fought amongst themselves for the privilege of going. He chose from among them a corporal and fourteen whom he saw to be the most determined. The corporal was Suceso Terrero, whose name was to shine in letters of gold in the book of the Legion. They knew that they were going to die. Before leaving, several of the soldiers made their last requests. One of them, Lorenzo Camps, had received his pay only a few days before, and had not yet spent any of it. He delivered the 250 pesetas to the officer, saying, 'My Lieutenant, since we are going to certain death, will you do me the favor of donating this money in my name to the Red Cross?'

"Night was falling when they reached the blockhouse. The enemy attacked it viciously; an enormous flash illuminated the blockhouse, and a loud crash brought several of its defenders to the ground. The Moors had brought up their cannon, and were bombarding the place furiously. In a few moments the blockhouse 'El Malo' had disappeared, its defenders buried beneath the debris."

Franco closed the account with the following comment: "This is how we defend a position! . . . This is how the Legionnaires die for Spain!" . . .

During those days two successful convoys were carried through, the memories of which were to echo in history. The first had the importance of a battle, and the fighting became so extended that the Legionnaires had to fight on four fronts, and in such critical straits at certain moments that in order to aid the position of Ait-Aisa, Captain Malagón was obliged to mobilize the Legionnaires and the stewards left in the camp, plunging with them into the battle, from which he came back gravely wounded. Three other officers of the Legion were also wounded that day.

The convoy of Casabona, on the 8th of September, was also epic. In order to thwart it, a great force, of proportions seldom seen before, was concentrated. Legionnaires and Regulars rushed to the attack. All the troops fought with courage that was exemplary. "The dead and wounded multiplied. The valiant Blanes," describes Franco, "the aristocrat from Granada, standard-bearer of the First Banner, fell at our feet mortally wounded. As they took him away he was crying, 'Long live Spain! Long live the Legion!'"

Lieutenant Sanz Prieto was taken away from the parapet, his face bloody, a bullet wound in the mouth. He began, "Long live the Le . . . !" He could not end it. Lieutenant Vila reached the ambulances with his arms mangled. The fighting continued. The commander of the Legion was forced to assume personal command of the entire line, for Lieutenant-Colonel González Tablas, who was in command of the Regulars, had been wounded. The tribute of the Legion on that day had not ended. Lieutenant Penche died of a bullet wound in the head while he manned a machine gun. Lieutenant Manso fell wounded also.

But the courage of the troops gradually shattered all resistance, and the convoy entered Casabona. General Sanjurjo, who had been living hours of anxiety, went out to await the return of the victors. In his emotion he embraced Franco.

The casualties of the Legion amounted to more than ninety, a third of the men who had begun the fighting. The official Army Report of the 10th of September says: "In the operations of the 8th at Casabona, the Foreign Legion and the Regulars from Ceuta, No. 3, once more had the occasion of covering themselves with glory. With their indomitable valor, with their admirable patriotism, with their incomparable skill, they succeeded in dealing the enemy one of the severest blows they have suffered in all our campaigns, causing them numerous casualties. . . ."

CHAPTER VII

The Reconquest of Melilla

ON THE first anniversary of the formation of the Legion, an almost legendary aureola of heroism surrounded it. Four months of war had been sufficient to win it. And of those four, half had been spent in engagements in the western zone that were so minor that they made mockery of the bravery of the Legion. But the two months of fighting which it had already spent in Melilla were good enough for the best history, and no more proof was required or needed to know what kind of a body the Legion was going to be.

On the other hand, less known was the fact that that spirit of sacrifice, the fighting morale, and that impetuous reaction in the face of danger, had not appeared spontaneously in the souls of those soldiers. Few thought of the leaders who had inculcated these qualities; energetic instructors; and above all, leaders who at the moment of putting their teachings into practice, confirmed them with an exemplary conduct, face to face with the enemy.

Millán Astray and Franco were chiefly responsible for creating the heroic atmosphere whence the military abilities of the Legion germinated and developed in abundance. Of those first volunteers — a heterogeneous conglomeration cast into enlistment by the ebb and flow of life — they made soldiers whose fame was to spread as far as that of the "grognards" of Napoleon, or the Prussian Grenadiers. Out of six months of solitude in the camp at Uad Lau had come the Legionnaires of "The Blockhouse of Death" and the convoy of Casabona, and the victorious battles which they were yet to wage, for the longed-for hour of the reconquest of the zone of Melilla was close at hand.

The preparation of the army of liberation had been slow and thorough. The High Commissary was proceeding with such caution that he irritated the impatient, who found "the tranquillity and passiveness of General Berenguer inexplicable." But the General knew everything that he was risking, and left nothing to chance. He gave out detailed information of his plans as they developed, not only to the generals that surrounded him, but to the government itself. Meanwhile Monte Arruit and Zeluán were wasting away in a siege that was to end in a massacre. Berenguer continued to check over the forces which were being sent to him. "This is a conglomeration of units, all deficient in equipment, training, and actual strength, for the battalions oscillate around 450 men with their companies of machine guns, and until this is organized and suitably prepared in every aspect, from that of command to that of marching equipment, we have no guarantee that the troops will be able to fight effectively. This is a truly extraordinary case, for it is a matter not of reinforcing an army with new men, but of creating an army to fight the next day."

At the end of August there were some 36,000 men in Melilla, but they lacked munitions, which were expected to arrive at any moment. The order to advance on Nador was not given until the middle of September. "The battle," says Franco, "is expected to be hotly contested, and the moments that separate us from the road to reconquest seem long."

At four in the morning on the 17th the First Banner left to concentrate in the Third Blockhouse. Three hours later the land and sea batteries opened fire. The explosions raised whirlwinds of smoke in the town, on the hills, and in the gaping fissures. The attack had begun. To the roar of the artillery was added the cracking of the rifles and the biting staccato of the machine guns.

Major Franco found himself in the front lines with his Legionnaires, preparing to cross a broad gulley and mount the hills of Nador. The entire zone was under the fire of the enemy. Millán Astray came to the advance posts to study the terrain. He approached Franco, who was standing next to the soldiers firing from the trench. The Commander of the Legion listened to the explanation which he gave him of the advance. In the next instant Astray dropped to the ground, raising his hands to his chest, where a bullet had caused a gush of blood. "Long live the Legion!" he cried. Franco helped to place him on a cot, but instantly he returned to his post, flourished his cane, and shouted, "Forward!" The Legionnaires crossed the gulley and swept to the top of the hills of Monte Arbos in a violent assault.

That night, on the way back to their camp, the Legionnaires traversed Nador, which was saturated with an intolerable stench. "The dead were piled in the houses and the courtyards. . . ." The reconquest had begun. Seven days later, in a new advance, the Spanish troops reached Tahuima and recovered the Fourth Blockhouse and the Airdrome.

At the start of the offensive, the enemy, who seemed somewhat lethargic, and very busied with the enjoyment of the booty yielded to them by the disaster of Annual, was startled, fearful that the Spanish troops would turn up among the tribes which they considered inexpugnable. The ringleaders rode over the territory inciting the tribes to war, and in a short time impressive arrays of warriors had gathered before the Spanish front. From the neighborhood of Sebt alone "5,000 men were assembled, and the presence of Riffians gave them a more aggressive propensity." The concentration at Segangan was made up of more than 3,500 fighters of the Riff.

The advance toward Sebt was considered "as one of the most delicate and difficult operations imposed by the reconquest, not only in the conditions of the terrain, favorable to the enemy, but also by being the point where the latter could concentrate great contingents of men with convenient approaches for their assembly or dispersion. In order to estimate its importance, it is enough to point out that the control of these approaches would give us possession of Gurugú."

On the first of October this operation was carried out. Sanjurjo's column, in which were incorporated Franco's Legionnaires, had as its task the occupation of the ancient position of Ulad-Dau, on the plateau of the same name.

The battle which was begun at dawn, did not end until night. The enemy knew well what was at stake, and held out to the death without retreating. Abd-el-Krim himself was at the head of his troops, some of whom were dressed in khaki and maneuvered in European fashion. "A hard day and a real battle," said the High Commissary, "but also a day of glory for our arms; not only in the bravery with which the troops fought, successful in defeating a numerous enemy who yielded no ground until we were face to face with them, but also in the precision with which the columns maneuvered, and the skill demonstrated by their commanders."

Franco set down the inventory of the Legion's losses on this day in his diary: Lieutenant Agulla, gravely wounded; Lieutenant Urzáiz, gravely wounded; Captain Franco Salgado, wounded; Lieutenant España, wounded; Lieutenant Calvacho, twice wounded; Lieutenant Montero, gravely wounded; one hundred forty-three casualties among the troops.

During the thickest of the fighting, when Major Franco was approaching the Regulars of Ceuta, who were meeting stiff resistance to co-ordinate the advance, he saw the lieutenant-colonel who led them in place of González Tablas fall wounded. That Lieutenant-Colonel of the Regulars was Emilio Mola.

From this moment onward the operations developed smoothly, with brief intervals of calm in order to consolidate the gains. The victory of Sebt was followed by the occupation of Atlaten. The First and Second Banners attacked the ancient fortress and nailed their colors at the top of the central fort. At the foot of the flags lay dying the Legionnaire who had affixed one of the banners. Towering and athletic, he was a Negro.

The encampment of Segangan was reconquered in military stride; the consequences of the triumph of Sebt. The enemy had fallen back toward Gurugú in search of a place of refuge and natural defensive barriers, and the troops were forced to dislodge them from the gulleys and the cliffs, where the bands had raised pieces of artillery, with which they were harassing the city of Melilla. The operation was carried out on the 10th of October, "a glorious day," in the words of Franco, in the history of the Legion.

The column of Sanjurjo, in which were the two Banners, was entrusted with the occupation of Taxuda, in order to hold back the forces of the enemy who would gather there to prevent the advance of the rest of the columns. As soon as Hardú, Basbel, and Takigriat had been occupied, Sanjurjo's column was to begin its retrenchment, which had to be performed with infinite care and precaution. The concentration of the troops was effected during the night. At sunrise, Sanjurjo, in pajama shirt, and mounted on his horse, inspected his troops.

The Legionnaires had to take possession of some peaks of porous rock infested with enemy soldiers. But that was not all. These soldiers formed the protection for the main body of the forces, which unleashed all its offensive fury against the column of Sanjurjo. And soon the battle reached its maximum intensity. The stretcher-bearers came and went from the battle lines to the ambulance station. "The tribesmen fought as never before." While the other columns accomplished their tasks with relative ease and reached the summits of Gurugú, Sanjurjo's column had to bear up in a desperate effort under the Riffian cyclone, which wanted to break through the blockade at any cost to attack the Spanish troops in the rear.

Sanjurjo's column was being decimated. The Battalion of the Princess was left without officers. Captain Cobos, of the Legion, the "ace of the machine gunners," fell with a bullet through his abdomen.

"What happened?" Franco asked him.

"Nothing! Nothing!" answered the captain, his eyes glazed with death.

The enemy were attacking from all sides. Appeals for aid came incessantly. Franco was present everywhere. From the left sector they asked him for reinforcements. When he visited the line occupied by the Sixth Company of Machine Gunners, he was asked for a protection of Legionnaires, because the enemy were almost upon them. "Into the threatened posts," says Franco, "we poured our men and our courage. . . . The enemy hurled themselves upon us fearlessly. The moral coefficient of the Peninsular troops was surpassed, and the left front wavered at certain points."

Night fell, and the battle continued more furiously than at its beginning. As there was a shortage of men, even the muleteers had to abandon their mules to take up positions in the front lines. The enemy were clinging to the Spanish vanguards, and retreat was difficult.

Franco ordered the placing of some machine guns from another body to protect the retrenchment. His aide, the Baron of Misena, returned and said that his orders had been carried out. They were his last words. In that instant he fell, his head shattered by a bullet.

Two soldiers of the guerrilla took his lifeless body to the ambulance post, where lay the bodies of Lieutenants Moore and Rodrigo, Legionnaires, and where Lieutenant Echevarría, adjutant to the Second Banner, soon arrived, his face bloody. There was an endless line of stretchers. The chaplain, with his stole over his shoulders, bent over each wounded or dying man and absolved him. The stretcher-bearers drew away with their sorrowful burden.

The troops reached Atlaten at night, while the artillery lighted up swift flashes in the mountains, and the thunder of the explosions rolled forth with the dull murmur of a stormy sea.

That night Melilla celebrated its liberation; Gurugú had ceased being a worry and a haunting apparition.

CHAPTER VIII

The Road to Annual

THE Legion convalesced in the encampment. It had lost more than half of its personnel and needed to reorganize. It filled its ranks with volunteers from Ceuta, men without the indispensable military training, and whom it was necessary to instruct.

During the last two weeks of October, Zeluán and Monte Arruit were conquered. There was no great resistance on the part of the enemy.

Zeluán! Monte Arruit! A Via Dolorosa for Spain. The road to Annual. The road of disaster. The fields, full of unburied dead, with the signs of martyrdom. The walls, with stains that would never fade away, epitaphs traced by the fires in which were burned the corpses. All that was left of an army in defeat: coats and bandages torn from the wounded; flocks of ravens circling over that feast of carrion and misery. With the troops arrived the relatives of some of those martyrs, in whom the power of pity and love revealed less than the tragic truth before their eyes. They tried to identify their own!

Spain, through her soldiers, expiated those profanations and that ignominy, giving to the dead the peace denied them by the tribesmen.

Major Franco threw his handful of earth on the graves of the anonymous martyrs of the disaster of 1921.

In the month of November the operation on Taxuda was repeated, in order to occupy certain positions of great strategic value and indispensable for future operations.

The Legionnaires were already acquainted with that road that led up to the porous rocks overlooking Telat. The First Banner had been reinforced with numerous South American volunteers, who were eager to take part in the fighting.

And the initial engagement was not exactly a sham battle. They had to use their bayonets several times, leaping among the rocks. Sergeant Herben, of the Second Company, fell headlong from a cliff, locked in struggle with a Moor. Soon after, another sergeant, faithful to the Legionary tradition of never abandoning a wounded or a dead comrade on the field, recovered the body. Captain Fortea, of the police, who was serving as Franco's aide, fell with a bullet through his chest.

The triumph was swift, for the enemy did not resist the spirited thrust of the Spanish troops. General Cavalcanti and his General Staff, who had witnessed the operation, congratulated Major Franco when he arrived. "This is the greatest day in the history of the Legion, he exaggerated.

Franco later remarked, "I think it was the first day they observed us at close range."

The cold made its appearance. Torrential rains, that left the roads mired with a reddish clay, burst on the encampment at Segangan. They were gray days and icy nights, interminable, in constant alarm, for the camp was dominated by the imposing hulk of Mount Uisán, like the wall of an invulnerable citadel. On the heights were the fortlets of the Moorish guards, and under cover of night the Moorish snipers slipped out to harass the encampments and positions. The conquest of this natural fortress, with its savage peaks, its vertical fissures and its ravines, would require a slow and expensive operation. Aside from the fact that the enemy saw themselves very well protected in their resistance, the aid of artillery could not be relied upon, for the reason that it would be useless to pit the cannons against those huge masses of living rock.

There was, however, one way of conquering Uisán: a surprise attack by night. And such an idea naturally arose in the minds of the Legionnaires. Franco laid out the plan before the General, and the latter approved it. "In case the weather prevents us from going to Ras Medua, we shall take Mount Uisán."

The preparation of the surprise attack required study; a knowledge of the positions where the enemy had their lairs; a knowledge of the trails leading to them, and preparation for retreat in case the thrust failed. The labor was carried out in great secrecy.

Major Franco cautioned all those taking part in the feat. The rifles were to be carried under the coats so that the bolts would not rattle. No one was to smoke, or fire his arms. The machine guns were to be carried. The munitions also were to be carried in the arms of thirty men.

The departure was at dawn. Before separating, Franco made sure through the captains and lieutenants that each man knew his respective task. And they went forth to the deed, to the great hope that was already the restless dream of all the Legionnaires involved in the extraordinary enterprise of the seizure of Mount Uisán.

The foreman of the Compañía Española de Minas del Riff acted as guide. The Legionnaires filed along, like a procession of phantoms. They did not walk. They glided along, clinging to the slopes, creeping on all fours through the ravines, bent over and silent as they filed through the clefts of the torrential gorges. Night and silence. "Not the slightest sound was to be heard; not a single shout had betrayed our presence." The Legionnaires continued, climbing ever upwards.

With the first sight of dawn, Franco noticed a thin column of smoke that ascended and spread out, like a fine gauze. It was the sentry of the fortlet of San Enrique. "There is not another minute to lose." What moments of emotion they must have felt as they mounted the last slope!

Shots flashed out in the dim morning light. The Moorish sentries, surprised, attempted to rally, and then, from among those rocky spots of fearful solitude the Legionnaires surged forth as at a magic word, inflamed with passion. Forward! The intruders took possession of the fortlet.

The sun of that day wrapped in its first gold the Spanish flag above the highest peak of Beni-bu-Ifrur.

The operations carried out during the following days developed with more ease, since the enemy, each time more crushed, lessened its resistance. The new Commander-General of Melilla, Sanjurjo, who had substituted General Cavalcanti, was entirely familiar with the territory in which he had served from the beginning of the campaign of reconquest. He took charge and resumed the advance on the objectives that constituted the enlargement already agreed upon, occupying Tauriat Zag and Tauriat Buchi on the 20th, in order to close the Masin valley; he also occupied Uld-el-Mir and Kudia Luta, on the Garet front, to prepare the thrust to Batel. On the 21st, Batel and Tistutin were occupied. On the 22nd, Sanjurjo proceeded to cross the Kert over the bridge on the road to Kaddur, meeting stiff resistance, which he overcame with less than a hundred casualties. Franco led the shock troops. On that same day he occupied Kaddur, Kalukl, and Ras Tikermin. In less than three months the entire program of the year 1909 and a great part of the program of the years 1911 and 1912 had been carried out.

Those who thought that the Kert River was to be the frontier that would hold back the advance were surprised at the new drive in the operations. Where were these Spanish troops going? The question aroused bitter polemics in the Peninsula, and the campaign in Morocco came to be once more the axis of politics.

"From Spain," General Berenguer wrote, "came rumors of a change in the situation, of malaise, of dissatisfaction with the campaign and its commander, rumors all that unnerved the troops and made the action of the High Command more difficult. The Minister of War himself and those who accompanied him on a recent trip to Melilla were able to observe how this propaganda was being spread throughout the army engaged in operations. There was also talk of the repatriation of units, which awakened uneasiness theretofore dormant or not felt.

"The initial impulse, which had made the campaign of reconquest begin under such favorable auspices, was being lost by giant strides."

With this unwillingness and uncertainty in higher circles, which fortunately did not reach the men in the front lines who had the enemy before their eyes, new operations were carried out at the beginning of the new year of 1922. General Sanjurjo, through two vigorous and brilliant advances, recovered Dar Busada and Dar Azugag on the 9th of January, and on the 10th Dar Drius, which, occupied for the first time in May of 1920 and lost on July 23 of 1921, was recovered six months after having been evacuated by the garrison of Melilla.

Dar Drius! Another name in the series of solemn and oracular epitaphs that marked like the Stations on the Way of the Cross the Calvary leading to Annual. From a great distance Franco's Legionnaires had a presentiment of what was in store for them, through the stench, the last cry for succor of the forsaken dead. If cruelty required a monument to mark the culmination of its rage, that monument would have to be conceded to Dar Drius, which in January of 1923 offered that hair-raising sight from which Franco drew his Legionnaires away, to spare them, together with sorrow, the exasperation of a desire for vengeance.

What infamy and what tragedy! And what suffering endured by those Spaniards, left unprotected in the days of July, when they were traversing these roads, enveloped in clouds of dust, maddened with thirst, blinded by the glare of the African sun, and pursued relentlessly by blood-intoxicated hordes!

Overwhelmed by that sight, Franco's military spirit quickly came to the surface, and he asked himself, at the sight of that plain, "an ideal terrain for fighting": "How was it that the sad retreat did not stop in Drius? The more we advance, the less explicable become the things that happened."

And following that he wrote some lines in which his thoughts became clearer, even though his pen checked them: "Traverse these fields; talk with the soldiers and petty officers who shared in the disaster, and question the natives; then only will you find the key to that retreat, which began in Annual, and ended in the massacres of Zeluán and Monte Arruit."

Six months after the tragedy of Annual, Spain paid little attention to events in Morocco, apparently being more concerned with what was happening on the other side of the Straits. The fact was that Morocco turned out to be the best topic for political maneuvers of every kind, to plot a crisis as well as to promote high-aspiring revolutionary propaganda. "In Madrid above all, the excitement produced by difference of opinion on the situation reached its peak; the campaigns, their results, the purposes, the aptitudes, and the methods followed were the subject of public discussion; some wished to continue it; others to consider it ended; some considered it imprudent to have crossed the Kert; others argued heatedly over the incompetence of the High Command, which had not yet conquered all the Riff territory; the system followed was discussed; some argued with overwhelming Napoleonic maxims: swiftness, mass, to seek the enemy wherever he is, and crush him; some based their arguments on the lessons of the ancient African wars, or wielded the moral maxims of the last century; teachings, arguments, and theories, which they thrashed out in public as the supreme science of triumph."

Under these conditions, the task of those in command in Africa became quite thankless.

With the occupation of Dar Drius the cycle of operations approved by the government had been closed. Nevertheless, General Berenguer had proposed to the conference held in Pizarra the continuation of the advance until the tribe of Beni-Said and with it Mount Mauro, the bulwark of the region of the Kert, were within the Spanish lines, and occupying a front extending from Drius through Ichtinen and Tuguntz, that would seek the position of Timayast by way of the sea, a line which could be advanced further, if political circumstances permitted, to Afrau.

On March 18 the great maneuver for the occupation of the plateau of Arkab and the domination of the plateau of Tikermin was being carried out, at the same time that an ample field for maneuvering was being assured for the occupation of Tuguntz and Dar Quebdani, and with it the most extensive and populated portion of Beni-Said, where Mount Mauro is situated.

Because of the stanch resistance offered by the enemy, Tuguntz, the objective, could not be occupied that day. The vanguards had to take up positions and fortify themselves half way to Tuguntz, on some hills where a town called Anvar was located.

And there they stayed, while General Sanjurjo sent an urgent call to Franco, who was at that time in the Peninsula, and who took command of the spearhead of the advance on the same day of his arrival in Dar Drius by airplane. The operation was carried out with such success, that after surprising the enemy and putting them to flight, all the objectives which could not be attained in the preceding operation were achieved, with a minimum number of casualties.

While the work of fortification was going on in the

new positions, Franco, who was scanning ceaselessly with
the aid of his binoculars the different sectors of the front,
noticed that a strange phenomenon was occurring on a
certain hill. The Regular force, hard-pressed, were beginning to retreat. He saw something else. He saw how
they were carrying back on a stretcher the commanding
officer of the Regulars, identifying him by means of the
cap that he held between his hands. Franco understood all,
and with that rapidity of judgment peculiar to him he
hastened on horseback to the place where confusion and
panic were disarticulating the front line, to take over their
leadership, restoring them to their fighting posts with cries
and impulsive courage. The situation was saved, and the
day, which could have been fatal, ended victoriously.

At the hour of retreat, Major Fontanes, who commanded
the Second Banner throughout the entire campaign, fell
with a bullet through his abdomen.

Fontanes knew fully the seriousness of his wound.
"Pagés will save me," he gasped. But Doctor Pagés was
far away, and the major died at dawn. "The Legion is in
mourning," said Franco, "it has lost one of its best officers.
The soldiers are sad, but they do not weep, for in their eyes
there are no tears left. They have seen so many of their
officers and comrades fall."

In the month of April Dar Quebdani was occupied.
With this occupation could be considered ended the
maneuver on Beni-Said, which closed the new frontier
between Dar Quebdani and the sea, and the boundary of
Alcazaba Roja, which assured the domination of Mount
Mauro. It was the last of the active and important operations in the zone of Melilla. In less than a month a tribe
had been dominated, that of Beni-Said, which before had
required ten years to subdue.

General Berenguer commented, "This important event
passed completely unnoticed in Spain, where it was received
coldly, few being aware of its significance, which was

nothing less than the consummation of our objectives in the territory of Melilla and the final point of the advance."

Major Franco was decorated with the Military Medal, the highest distinction next to the Cross of San Fernando.

CHAPTER IX

Franco, Commander-in-Chief of the Legion

THERE was no peace in Morocco, no matter how much the government toiled to obtain it, not even when, as proof that the war was declining, twenty thousand soldiers were discharged from Africa. There was no peace, not even after the line of positions in Melilla that held back the advances had been established. Spain had reached that line, and beyond it she would not pass, it was said. But the Moors did not care to understand such prohibitions; and the Raisuni, with the assistance procured for him by the brother of Abd-el-Krim, kept in arms the warriors of Beni-Arós, against whom the High Commissary, Dámaso Berenguer, who awaited only to arrive in Tazarut to consider his mandate in Africa ended, now directed his columns.

The operations were unfolded in the mysterious mountains of Yebala, never before conquered, under torrential rains. Those painful marches were not without their reward. On the 12th of May, 1922, the Spanish troops entered Tazarut and broke the secret of the refuge of the Raisuni, lord of the mountains of Beni-Arós, who, from those magnificent buildings decorated in oriental taste and surrounded by gardens, radiated his despotic power to all the lands of Yebala. But the victory was garnished with a bow-knot of crepe. There died González Tablas, that great soldier, first in combat, the meteor of the war, who was killed also by his great love of Africa.

When this advance had been accomplished, the government did not allow the operation to be rounded out, because it was determined upon putting an immediate end to the Moroccan business. It insisted that the discharge of soldiers be hastened, as if it were convinced that the sooner the troops returned to Spain, the sooner the war would end. This procedure was like burying one's head in the sand, and could not give good results.

Then came an unfortunate period for Spain's action in Africa. High Commissaries, now civilians, followed each other in rapid succession, as well as commanding military officers; all, after a few months of residence in the zone, resigned as soon as they came face to face with the terrible reality of the problems of the war, which were impossible of solution by a precarious, diminished, and mediocre authority like that which they had received.

To be sure, some troops had been repatriated; lines of the nature of immovable frontiers had been marked out, beyond which it was forbidden to advance. But the enemy, who did not ignore conditions in the Peninsula, would not agree to maintain themselves impassive and respectful before the Spanish positions. They attacked them whenever they could, destroying the plans laid out in Madrid for the permanent frontiers, and obliged the Spaniards to change their lines frequently and mark them out with blockhouses and camps which were merely so many more challenges to the fury of the tribesmen.

One of the commanding officers proposed to enter Beni-Urriaguel by another road, and with this in mind the troops occupied the salient of Tizzi-Assa, which threatened the enemy through the two furthest positions of Midar and Afrau. It was thought that there the advance to invade the territory of Abd-el-Krim would be begun some day. The position was on the summit of a bare and savage mountain, with the knifelike prow of an armored cruiser. But Tizzi-Assa was a hell. Harassed day and night by rifle and cannon fire, it held out with a prodigious heroism.

Frequently besieged, to lift its blockade required necessarily a severe battle, the tragic exchange of blood for food and water. What a sad fame that of the convoys of Tizzi-Assa! A solution of the problem by a series of operations implied a concentration of troops. None of the High Commissaries who succeeded each other from May of 1922 to June of 1923 was considered endowed with the ability necessary for this task.

But in this month the urgency was so pressing that it allowed of no delays. The enemy took up such strategic positions that they made access to the summit impossible. Tizzi-Assa, besieged, would succumb, and the Moors awaited its fall as the promise of another calamity like that of 1921. The Banners of the Legion that were fighting in the zone of Larache were brought to Melilla at full speed, arriving with the dust of Beni-Arós on their boots. The Legionnaires know no rest.

Rafael Valenzuela was Commander of the Legion, having been in command of it since Millán Astray was forced to abandon his post because of his wounds. Valenzuela, "one of the best soldiers in the army," in the words of Alfonso XIII, belonged to that heroic body of colonial officers formed in the war. He was tall, strong, and noble in character. A man with a pistol at his belt, which he grasped only in critical moments, like a scepter. His valor had an athletic gracefulness. A volunteer for the war, he maintained in battle the imperturbable countenance of one who is master of all his actions.

He was in Madrid when there began to be talk of the difficult situation of Tizzi-Assa, and he left hastily to occupy his post. Soon after he arrived in camp, without having taken any rest, he presented himself before Colonel Gómez Morato, who was in command of the column which included the Legion. The colonel informed him of the projected operation, and of the task allotted to the Legionnaires. Gómez Morato was laying excessive value on the promises given him by some *caídes* through spies that the troops would not find much resistance, as this had been overcome by certain types of propaganda.

The Commander of the Legion, less credulous, did not agree with the estimates of the colonel; but as the latter insisted, Valenzuela came out of the tent greatly worried and with a misgiving so profound that at one o'clock in the morning it forced him to his tent where a chaplain was sleeping, to ask, "Father, I should like to have you hear my confession, because in a few hours I am going to die."

This request, at such an unusual hour, surprised the priest, and he inquired after the reasons, but Valenzuela fell contritely on his knees as a sole answer.

At daybreak he left for Tahuarda with the mission of clearing the road. Everything occurred exactly as his heart and his intellect had foreseen. That was his final battle. Hardly had he started on the road that ascended to Benítez, when the enemy opened fire, heavy, concentrated, unremitting. The tribesmen, well hidden in the ravines, were drawing the Spanish troops onward to surround them. On reaching Peñas de Tahuarda, there was produced an instant of indecision, which Valenzuela resolved by rushing forward to the attack in the lead to the cry of "Long live the Legion! Forward!" He carried his pistol in one hand, in the other his Legionnaire's cap. In that instant he fell forever, with a bullet in his chest and another in his head.

The Legion was left without a leader. Who was to take his place? The name was in the mind of everyone, with extraordinary unanimity: Franco! There was no doubt about it. The King himself acknowledged it in the following manner, "There is no one who surpasses him. It has to be Franco."

Franco had to be the leader of those veteran troops, because his past compelled it. He was courage and daring united to brilliancy and will power. But once again arose the difficulty which was now traditional in the triumphal march of his life. That obstacle was his age. Franco was thirty years old and not yet a lieutenant-colonel. He lacked the rank, although there were several nominations for promotion in his favor. At the meeting of the Cabinet on June 7 his appointment as lieutenant-colonel was decided. It was the first promotion granted in the army during the period from 1921 to 1923.

Franco accompanied the body of Valenzuela to Zaragoza, where he was buried in the crypt of Our Lady of Pilar in the Cathedral with the honors merited by heroes. But he returned at once to his post. When the commander presented himself before his Legionnaires, they acclaimed him as their leader.

Franco was a veteran in the Legion. Rather, he was the first Legionnaire, and knew, therefore, the responsibilities inherent in the high position which had just been granted to him.

For their part, the Legionnaires recognized the fact that no one possessed the merits that Franco did to hold a position of leadership that belonged to him by right and by reason of courage, which was the supreme law of the Legion.

That courage, fundamental in the spirit of one who professes the creed of the Legion, that scorn of death in battle that is the aureola and the virtue of such a soldier, have not made of Franco a man without mercy, or deprived him of love and sympathy toward his fellow men.

He is a man who trains his warriors in energy, audacity, and fearlessness; when in camp he is troubled by the news of the illness of a soldier, hastens to the side of a wounded comrade, and takes intense interest in the tribulations and spiritual crises suffered by many of those men of shattered lives; men whose limbs have been wrecked by the storm, but whose spirits are sound, and sunk in a natural depth of kindness, eager to be reborn some day in a fair and luminous spring.

He treats his soldiers with the superior mastery of a leader. And he loves them as companions because he lives with them in those frontier zones of battle where the Fatherland ends and begins. With the soldiers he has shared the worries, the hardships, and the illusions of that life in the vanguard in which everything is lacking and in which everything seems superfluous. He has suffered the fire of burning days, and the snows and fog of winter, under a field tent like those of the soldiers or in the open air, identified with them through the same dangers and united to them by the same destiny.

That is why Franco is the perfect soldier, who wields over his troops an influence that brands them with the strength of a style. The style of the Legion, which is passed on and perseveres through years and vicissitudes, which is peculiar to that colonial infantry, and which other troops have imposed upon themselves as a model and have imitated when they wished to excel. A spirit that Franco saw dawn in Ceuta, beheld resplendent in Melilla and Tetuán, and for which he dreamed of a glory without end.

Among the memorable events of this first period as Commander of the Legionnaires stands out the liberation of Tifarauín, a position besieged by the enemy, and where the besieged were holding out with an indomitable spirit.

Franco had returned from a short trip to the Peninsula, and the news of his arrival had been transmitted to the defenders of the position by a message directed to the Second Lieutenant Topete, the leading spirit in the defense, in which was contained the following message: "Hold out for a few more hours. Franco is coming to your rescue."

The heliograph of Tifarauín palpitated with hope: "If Franco is coming, we shall hold out. Long live Spain!"

Franco planned the operation with the absolute certainty

of carrying it out successfully. He studied the terrain for many hours, and finally ordered that the troops take up posts in distant and dangerous parts of the position and seemingly seriously exposed. Those who were listening seemed not to understand him. But Franco, with a resolution that allowed no reply, said to them, "Be on your guard, and in a few hours you will have the entire enemy within reach of your rifles. I am going to attack them from the rear."

Everything happened as the Commander of the Legion had anticipated. Tifarauín was left free of pressure, and the enemy were decimated in their flight. The besieged recovered their liberty. Major Beorlegui was one of the first to enter the position. He carried in his hands a watermelon, to appease the thirst of the unconquerables of Tifarauín.

General Fernández Pérez, in speaking of the participation of Franco in the operations at Melilla, said:

"His extraordinary ability to lead troops commands attention. . . . He excels in the fulfillment of duty, and takes the initiative with certainty and assurance when the circumstances demand it, which are clear proofs of his worth, his attainments, and his sense of responsibility.

"Despite his youth, he has a cool, calm mind, is calculating in his decisions, and is calm in action, combining admirably these qualities, so valuable to a commanding officer, with his bravery, which leads him to examine operations from dangerous positions in order to base his decisions on personal observations, which are always well founded and in keeping with the exigencies and purposes of this war which he knows so well.

"We are dealing with a leader who always stands out, and who has displayed on many difficult occasions his qualities as a high commanding officer. For these reasons, and because I believe that it is the duty of the High Command to grant to Lieutenant-Colonel Francisco Franco

Baamonde the rewards which he so well deserves. I do honor to myself by proposing in this special manner, emphasizing the justice of my proposal, that he be given a raise in rank immediately."

On October 16, 1923, Franco went to the Peninsula to marry. Franco succeeded in realizing a desire which he had had to postpone upon two occasions because of the exigencies of war. His wife, Carmen Polo y Martínez Valdés, a daughter of a distinguished Asturian family, unites a suggestive beauty to her refined and cultured spirit and her graceful congeniality. They first met in early youth, and loved each other. She was then fifteen years old, and he was a little over twenty. She was tall and slender, with sweet and caressing eyes; her hair was parted in the middle, and fell down in long black tresses.

To what ingenuity they had to resort in order to see each other, subjected as the girl was to a strict paternal vigilance which was opposed to those relations! The love of joyful days of spring that is kept in the treasury of memories as the greatest gift of life. The young man awaited at the door of the school where she was being educated, to receive the glance that was a promise of fidelity and future.

A promise which persevered through distance, through long absences, through the vicissitudes of the life of a soldier, and through the opposition of some of the relatives of the bride, who tried to persuade her not to marry a fearless man who always lived so dangerously. But she followed her heart.

"In my home," she recalls today, "we were all then pacifists. A little later my father was following on the maps with passionate fondness the course of the African war in which Francisco was participating."

Her father, Felipe Polo y Flórez, a wealthy and well-known resident of Oviedo, was the son of Claudio Polo y Astudillo, Professor of Literature in the High School and the author of several excellent works. The mother of the bride belonged to old Asturian nobility.

The wedding was held in the Church of San Juan in Oviedo. Franco, who was lord of His Majesty's bedchamber, had as his best man the King, who delegated General Antonio Losada, Military Governor of Oviedo, to represent him.

At the end of a month Franco returned to his command in Africa.

CHAPTER X

Primo De Rivera and Morocco

THE Military Dictatorship had not yet completed its first year. Primo de Rivera, Marquis of Estella, had undertaken the great task of national reconstruction, after removing from power and reducing to silence the cliques of politicians that had scandalously divided the spoils of the nation, condemned to passion and death. But the Marquis of Estella soon began to feel the nuisance that fettered his steps, embarrassed his movements, distracted his attention, and distorted his designs. This nuisance was Morocco, the North of Africa, that threw forth ever its sinister shadow on the destinies of Spain. It was also an unwholesome and suffocating wind, that parched the hopes of the renascent nation and disturbed all Spaniards with uneasiness and fear.

The previous governments had thought that they could hold the troops on a line marking the extreme limit of advance, and leave the maneuvers of conquest to diplomacy, excluding as far as possible the use of arms.

Primo de Rivera, too, had suffered the contagion of this superstition. He presumed that a few skillful agents would subdue Abd-el-Krim and the Raisuni, even converting them into friends and allies of Spain. That was in keeping with a firm conviction of the Marquis that anything which could not be obtained in Morocco by persuasion, was useless, no matter how costly, to try to obtain by force; and that abandonment was even preferable. He solemnly asked for this upon two occasions, both times jeopardizing seriously the high offices that he held.

He now had absolute power, and before him the uncertain factor of the problem of Morocco, as victorious as ever, and absorbing all the attention, the wealth, and the energy which Spain could command. What was to be done?

Primo de Rivera, faithful to his convictions and resolute in his judgment, once again thought of abandonment. But power enslaves and binds with a strength unknown and never endured by those who live far removed from it. There were treaties that demanded fulfillment, and a network of interlocking interests, and a sea of blood already shed, and an army that refused to render sterile the sacrifices lavished so freely on African soil.

The solution came of its own accord, for the enemy began to exert pressure on the Spanish positions, attacking and surrounding them. "The state of affairs in the western zone has been aggravated considerably by the insurrection of some tribes, and the dubious attitude of others provoked by the presence of bands of Riffians from the Sierra de Gomara, which is making it difficult to supply and communicate with our positions."

Thus said a semiofficial note of July 1, 1924. But the whole truth was that an uprising of the tribes had begun in the western zone which was to attain greater proportions and importance, as Primo de Rivera admitted on another occasion, than that of 1921 in the zone of Melilla.

All the positions in the basin of the Lau were besieged, and aid to them was almost impossible because of their mountainous location, the distance, and the scarcity of troops. Once again the tragic anguish of a crumbling front. And as then, Franco with his Legionnaires, rushed hastily to the place of danger.

Blockhouses and positions resisted with an epic heroism. Forsaken among the mountains and forests of Beni-Said, of Beni-Hassan, and Gomara, beyond all hope of rescue, without food or water, they held out with the best Spanish bravery.

One of the positions in greatest danger was Koba Darsa, to which there had been made four useless attempts to send a convoy. In the office of the commanding officer at Tetuán there was opposition to the repetition of the attempt. There was no other solution, if it can be called thus, than to let it perish helplessly. But someone pointed out, "Why do we not summon Franco?"

Franco was with his Legionnaires far away in the position of "García Uría," in the Gomara mountains. But it was decided to notify him to come to Tetuán immediately. Franco understood the gravity of those summons and attended to them at once. At dawn he left the position on horse and descended to the Tetuán highway, where an automobile awaited him. At ten in the morning he was in the office of the High Commissary. A few words and all was clear. Koba Darsa was at the end of its strength.

"Do you believe it would be possible to aid it?"

"I am certain of it," answered Franco.

"What would you need?"

"You would have to give me ample powers to carry out the operation exactly as I plan it."

"You can count on them definitely. When will you need them?"

"Immediately. I need now a boat to take me to Uad Lau."

"It will await you in the Martín River."

At one o'clock in the afternoon Franco arrived in Uad Lau, surprising the generals assembled there, their spirits darkened by the shadow of Koba Darsa, which was wasting away in siege, beyond hope of aid, and beyond the possibility that any aid could be taken to it.

The Commander of the Legion explained: "We are going to rescue Koba Darsa."

The maps were on a desk, and Franco bent over them, with the eager eyes of a surgeon searching for an abscess. One of the officers at his side observed. "The river is impassible."

Franco, without lifting his eyes from the maps, answered him, "We do not have to cross the river."

In that very spot he dictated his orders, and warned the troops to get ready. He ordered specifically that no one should alter his instructions. He dictated to the artillery men when to lay down the protective barrages of fire.

Those assembled there looked at each other with surprise.

"But are we going to fight now?"

"Right now," Franco replied.

It was three o'clock in the afternoon in the month of July. No one ever thought of fighting in the most oppressive hour of the sun's heat. The land of Africa lay in silence, beaten down by that heat of molten lead. The troops began their march. A half hour later they were in contact with the enemy, who, surprised by the attack, hardly attempted to rally. At four thirty Koba Darsa, the impossible, was liberated. The maneuver was the work of an artist.

At nightfall Franco returned to Uad Lau. He asked for a glass of milk. It was the only food he had consumed for twenty hours. For when the day offers military adventure, and it is necessary to act, Franco forgets his meals.

The insurrection spread until it reached the gates of Xauen and Tetuán, cutting these cities off from communication and severing the road to Tangier.

Unexpectedly, Primo de Rivera, who wished to examine matters at close hand, left for Tetuán, and during his stay, some operations that temporarily relieved the situation were carried out. Communications were restored with Xauen and Tangier. The Marquis of Estella toured the territory and announced that in this as well as in the western zone there were positions that should disappear, being useless. He arrived in Melilla on the 18th of July, and almost at the same time Franco landed. By that time the rumor had spread that Primo de Rivera had the intention of retreating the positions of Beni-Said and Tafersit to the boundary of the Kert. "Spain," declared the Premier, "cannot continue to maintain her soldiers in isolated crags that cost so much trouble to supply. I have been confirmed in my convictions, which are the result of a conscientious study of the problem."

On his visit to Ben Tieb the Marquis of Estella was able to observe the reaction his plan had on the soldiers. Some significant posters at the entrance to the encampment expressed the fervent desire of the shock troops. "The Legion never retreats." The Banners were drawn up there with their Commander at their head. He delivered a speech of greeting.

"The soil we stand on, Mr. Premier," Franco said, "is Spanish soil, because it has been obtained at the highest price and paid for with the dearest of coin: Spanish blood.

"When we ask to go forward, it is not for our comfort and convenience, for we know well that in executing the order to advance we must serve in the vanguard, and that the road of conquest is watered by our blood and accompanied by the dead we leave by the wayside.

"We reject the idea of retreat, because we are convinced that Spain is now in a position to dominate the zone that belongs to it, and impose its authority in Morocco."

During the luncheon in honor of the distinguished guest, an incident occurred which would have been serious had Franco not intervened, succeeding in settling it amicably and skillfully to the satisfaction of all. But in case Primo de Rivera considered the occurrence deserving of sanction, the Commander of the Legion put his post at the visitor's disposal.

That night the President of the Military Directorate summoned Lieutenant-Colonel Franco to his office. That conversation was to leave an epoch-making mark in the annals of Spain. For the moment, there was to be no retreat in the zone of Melilla.

Franco invited Primo de Rivera to reflect on the advantages of going to Alhucemas. "The landing would be so easy, that it would put an end definitely to the Moroccan problem!"

The Marquis of Estella doubted it. Anyone who presumed as he did that the abandonment of Morocco would be a necessity that Spain could not avoid, would reject any advice that led to a perilous adventure. But Franco's voice that night pointed out the way and removed all obstacles. Alhucemas left the inaccessible and distant horizon and approached within their grasp — a prodigy of Franco's will power and conqueror's instinct. From that hour, Alhucemas remained a mirage toward which Primo de Rivera was to move insensibly as if driven by his destiny.

The President of the Directorate returned to Spain, and Franco to the western zone, where matters were not in a satisfactory condition. The insurrection was boiling in all its intensity in the month of August. The positions of Lau, Xauen, and those of the hulk of Gorgues were once again besieged, putting the security of Tetuán in imminent danger. "The news from Morocco," said a note of the twelfth of August, "is not satisfactory. . . . A general uprising of the tribes is to be seen in our zone as well as in the French."

Four columns, one of them led by Franco, carried out an operation through Beni-Hassam in order to punish the enemy and attract their attention, drawing them away from the positions they held beleaguered. They fought fiercely with well-equipped forces whose fighting morale was at a white heat.

Meanwhile the position of Chentafa had succumbed, with a tragic ending. For days and nights the garrison had resisted the attacks of a considerable force of the enemy. Seventeen of the defenders fell on one day alone. Chentafa lacked food and water and had only two cases of ammunition. The foe refused to desist from the attack, and there was no hope of rescue. The commanding officer of the position,

Lieutenant Vicente San José, was a man of extraordinary courage, who knew no surrender. He lacked equipment, and gradually, defenders. In his agony and the stubbornness of his resistance he determined on a plan of desperation. It was to set fire to the garrison. Before consummating his plan, he invited any of its defenders who so desired, to leave the position and flee. A little later Chentafa was burning, a gigantic pyre in which its defenders were destroyed. When the Moors entered the position, they found nothing but charred corpses amid a pile of smoldering ashes.

There was no end in sight to those fierce struggles borne by the Spanish columns, led by the best generals of the Spanish army, through ravines and over precipitous trails, under a torrid, asphyxiating, and ennervating sun. Battles that were made more painful by the torrential washouts that invaded the terrain, obstructing the roads and making natural trenches for the Moor.

Those feverish delays, those thickets, those solitudes, that abysmal emptiness, were filled with the anguished cries of the beleaguered positions, thirsty and delirious; voices of distress that the heart received, even though the ears heard them not. Drawn on by them went Franco with his Banners, with the intention of reaching them all, or at least of letting them know that they were not forsaken.

At the end of August, communication between Xauen and Tetuán was cut off. El Bakali betrayed the Spanish authorities and excited all the tribes of the Gomara mountains to rebellion. The positions on the Lau, many of them abandoned to their fate, were sacrificed in silence in the middle of the burning desolation of a Dantesque landscape. Some had lost even their heliographic communications. New pages of gold in the history of martyrs for the fatherland were written in silence.

Solano, defended by Lieutenant Rodríguez Urbano, was being consumed by thirst. The garrison had drunk two casks of vinegar and ended by drinking urine. In Dar Accoba, Lieutenant-Colonel Mola, at the head of the Regulars of Larache, began a defense which was to be memorable. The position of Buharrax was to endure forty-one days of siege; that of Seriya, defended by troops of the regiment from South America, seventy-three.

On the 5th of September the Directorate announced in a note "that it has considered it justified, in view of the nature of its personnel, to move in part to Tetuán in order that the difficulties which might arise could be solved more quickly and with a greater understanding of the causes." Generals Jordana, Muslera, and Rodríguez Pedret accompanied Primo de Rivera. The Marquis of Estella, "with a gesture of undeniable arrogance and determination, named himself High Commissary and commander-in-chief of all the troops in order to carry out under his direction the retreat of the Spanish forces in Yebala, without desisting in his idea, despite the opposition of the technical experts and the example of the reverses suffered."

Primo de Rivera's project included the abandonment of all the positions in the Yebala and Gomara mountains in order to maintain the occupation of what people were wont to call "Useful Morocco," which was a coastal fringe that included the highway from Tetuán to Tangier and Larache and another which insured the Ceuta-Tetuán highway.

The first communique that Primo de Rivera sent to Tetuán, on the 10th, reads thus: "Last night, after four hours of intensive work, M'Ter was evacuated. The plan of the Directorate, therefore, is thus beginning to be realized under the most favorable auspices."

CHAPTER XI

The Retreat from Xauen

PRIMO DE RIVERA realized that the most important thing to do was to relieve Tetuán of the danger that hovered over the city and open the road to Xauen, which had been severed by the rebellion of the Moors of Beni-Ider. The positions of Gorgues, which were the key to Tetuán, were enduring a siege that had lasted twenty days. If they succumbed, the road leading to the city would be left open to the enemy. Five columns were organized, one of which was under the command of Franco, who had just arrived in Tetuán, after having covered the retreat of the positions of the Tiguisas group. The operation lasted two days and two nights, "which the troops had to spend among cliffs, scaling and capturing them, enveloped by fog and damp cold." Beni-Hosmar was finally subdued, and Tetuán, relieved of the pressure that was strangling it, once more breathed freely.

A little later the mission of succoring Xauen was entrusted to General Castro Girona. In the vanguard of the column went the Legionnaires commanded by Franco. They opened the road that serpentined through defiles at bayonet point as they went along. On September 28th they reached Zoco de Arbaa, and on the 29th they entered Xauen. Almost at the same time the evacuation of the positions of "García Acero" and "Tahar-Berda" had been carried out in the Zoco el Jemis sector of Beni-Arós, under the protection of a battalion from Luchana. The battle sustained with the enemy was so severe that sixty per cent of the officers were lost, including Lieutenant-Colonel Andrade, and forty per cent of the troops.

For almost a month and a half Castro Girona's column, in which Franco's troops were incorporated, stayed in Xauen. The Legionnaires spent their time relieving some positions and evacuating others, taxing their ingenuity in order to remove the garrisons, and deceiving the foe through a thousand cunning stratagems. At the same time the departure of the ten thousand men making up the garrison of Xauen was being meticulously prepared, for they were surrounded on all sides by enemy forces awaiting the moment of retreat in order to fall upon them.

Meanwhile, the positions were gradually being dragged toward zones of safety. Some places were reached just in time to witness the agony of the survivors. The defenders of Nauer were carried out on litters, those of Abada Bajo were sick with malaria, and those of Buharrax were taken out in ambulances.

The hour of the greatest emotion was approaching, the sensational hour known only to the commanding officers and which was kept in secret, that of the departure from Xauen.

"What days of dreadful anxiety and hours of uncertainty and mortal fear for us who held the responsibility of command, and on whom so many lives depended!" Castro Girona was to exclaim.

On the night of November 15 the Spanish troops, leaving with the greatest secrecy, abandoned Xauen. The five Banners of the Legion under the command of Franco remained in the city, living an ordinary life.

"We must give the impression that we are never going to leave here," said Franco.

For two days the soldiers made dummies, stuffing Legionnaires' uniforms with straw. These dummies were placed on the parapets and stationed at strategic places. From a distance these insensible and immobile sentries appeared to the enemy to be Legionnaires at their posts of duty. They were the defenders that Franco had contrived in order to safeguard his soldiers from the risks of the departure.

At midnight on the 17th he gave the order to quit Xauen. The companies left silently in formation. Thus Franco abandoned the city with the last Legionnaires without firing a shot.

At dawn, the Moors who crowded the tops of the hills along the road harassed the Legionnaires until their arrival in Dar A Kobba. The Commander of the Legion maintained his poise and serenity, which were his characteristics even in that atmosphere of sorrow, for a piece of work that had cost immense sacrifices was crumbling to naught.

"With what sorrow have I said good-by to Xauen," he said to his companions.

How difficult it must have been for a warrior to maintain that cool and unchangeable tranquillity in those torturous hours, when he went forth into the field of battle not to gather laurels but to shatter them, not to extend his conquests but to reduce territory won through so much effort. But Franco fought with the same daring and the same faith as in days of glory, for it is in adversity that the temper of souls is proved.

On the following day the second stage of the retreat, from Dar A Kobba to Cheruta, was carried out under the protection of the Legionnaires, who occupied the heights on both flanks. By three o'clock in the afternoon all the troops of Castro Girona's column were entering Cheruta. They encamped there. During the night there was a torrential downpour of rain. Nevertheless, the retreat was continued, and on the following day Castro Girona's column reached Zoco de Arbaa in the middle of a furious rainstorm, which added tragedy to the retreat. Castro Girona's column was followed by that of General Serrano Orive, who came from Dar A Kobba through muddy roads. The hurricane wind enveloped the soldiers in a veritable avalanche of sheets of rain.

Thus they marched, their steps shackled by the mud, whipped by the deluge, exhausted by fatigue and long sleepless nights out in the open. The baggage was soaked. The cannons were continually getting stuck in the mire. The trucks would sink to their axles in the mud puddles. The ambulances, with their loads of feverish patients and the wounded were unable to advance in that confusion of men, cannons, and mules. And this entire march was proceeding amid the gunfire of the battles that were being fought by Franco's Legionnaires on the heights, at the full mercy of the elements, against the enemy that made every effort to fall upon that army that faded away through the mist and rain, in exodus, as a people fleeing from a cataclysm.

Thus the storm-beaten troops entered Zoco de Arbaa. That day's balance was sorrowful indeed. General Serrano Orive was killed by a sniper. Lieutenant-Colonel Temprano of the Regulars died also. General Federico Berenguer, Colonels Alvarez Arenas and Losada, and a goodly number of officers, for the most part from the Legion, were wounded.

In Zoco de Arbaa the troops had to hold out for three months, repulsing the great forces of Moors that persisted with such determination in their intent to convert the retreat into a disaster. They began to consider very seriously the impossibility of leaving Zoco de Arbaa in order to carry out the last stage of the retreat to Tarames and Ben Karrich.

In the face of that danger and uncertainty, and since the situation permitted no new delays, Franco demanded the honor of staying with the Legionnaires to defend the position, which was granted him. The battalions departed, and finally the Banners, who had to fight a stubborn battle with the enemy who refused to reconcile themselves to losing that opportunity of a colossal triumph with splendid booty.

The retreat from Xauen had ended. The most arduous undertaking, according to the estimate of the president *ad interim* of the Directorate, Magaz, ever accomplished by a colonial army, and in which more than a hundred positions were saved. While marching through the streets of Tetuán the Legion experienced one of its most resplendent hours of glory. The crowds followed Franco persistently, showering him with a triumphal thunder of cheers and ovations. For merits of war he was promoted to the rank of colonel.

Primo de Rivera was to say in praise of him, while speaking with a foreign news correspondent, "No one has fought more, nor with greater perseverance, nor with greater ability in Morocco."

Abd-el-Krim, gaining confidence by the retreat from Xauen, proclaimed himself Sultan of Morocco. He ruled over forty tribes. He held the Raisuni a prisoner in his power. He had the support of some international revolutionary organizations. He dreamed, as one delirious, of an empire extending from Axdir to Agadir and with his capital at Fez. And in the flight of his ambitions he stumbled into the French zone.

In the spring of 1925 the Riffs had invaded Beni-Zerual at five points. And once they were in control they attacked Uazan and the Uarga zone, where rebellion broke out. At the same time France suffered the crumbling of her positions and met the Calvary of sieges and treachery. It was a hurricane of disaster which demolished everything in its path. The Riff offensive threatened Fez. Painlevé, Minister of War, notifying the Treasury Department of French casualties up to July 31, gave the following figures: one thousand two hundred and eighty-five dead, including eighty-five officers, and five thousand three hundred and six wounded, one hundred and sixty of whom were officers.

Marshal Petain arrived at Robat as Inspector-General of the Army of Morocco, studied the situation, and concluded that "to solve definitely the Riff problem" it was necessary to collaborate with Spain. They came to an agreement. In an interview between the marshal and General Primo de Rivera the plan was worked out. It consisted of a series of operations in which the landing of the troops at the bay of Alhucemas was essential, in which action a division of the French navy was to co-operate.

The problem of Alhucemas was at last definitely solved. The control of Beni-Urriaguel had always been considered as necessary to assure the pacification of Morocco. Since 1911 the landing at Alhucemas had been the obsession of all those who were concerned with re-solving the African problem.

In 1922 Franco wrote in his *Diario de una Bandera:* "Alhucemas is the focal point of the rebellion against Spain, it is the road to Fez, the short cut to the Mediterranean, and there is to be found the center of much propaganda which will come to an end the moment we set foot on those coasts."

During Primo de Rivera's stay in Tetuán, and in the following months the president of the Directorate frequently discussed the problem of the conquest of Alhucemas with the military leaders who visited him. Far from being frightened by the project, he took pleasure in resting in his study complacently examining the possibilities of its realization. The general was surrounded by both the most fervent supporters of the plan and the pessimists who were combating it with all their strength. Primo de Rivera threw his lot with the former, and finished by acquiring a blind faith in the triumph of the project. His conversations with Franco gave him the most encouragement and so he sought him out.

"I am told," he expounded one day, "that the Alhucemas affair might be our ruin, that it is almost impossible."

"If we may count upon valor, which cannot possibly be lacking," answered Franco, "it is of mathematical certainty."

"However, they remind me of the English disaster at the Dardanelles."

"Those who speak that way do not want Spain to triumph, and they are unworthy of the glory of Alhucemas, which is certain. . . ."

"Certain . . . certain," repeated Primo de Rivera with diffidence.

"General," Franco affirmed, "the country would not forgive you if you did not end the Moroccan problem, and the key to that problem is Alhucemas. If you do not do it, my general, someone else will, because it is not only possible but it is necessary, and you will lose the success and glory that await you there for the welfare of Spain."

CHAPTER XII

The Landing at Alhucemas

IT WAS decided to go to Alhucemas. "However the idea of landing at Alhucemas may have originated, undoubtedly, and it is only just to recognize the fact, the will to carry it out was entirely that of General Primo de Rivera, then in control of the government and general in command of the African Army. . . . Entirely his, maintained tenaciously against the opinion and belief of everyone, and even with our allies lacking confidence in its success."

The columns for the landing were organized in Ceuta and Melilla. What hardships were undergone making preparations! The plan was to occupy a base of operations where an army of twenty thousand men could be handled. And at that base everything was lacking, from water to the most insignificant yet indispensable elements of life.

Ships, war materials, and men were being gathered. There arrived at the ports of Ceuta and Melilla warships, transports, trans-Mediterranean steamers, barges, and some original vessels called "Kaes," which had already been used by the English in their landing at the Dardanelles. These congregated troops of intendants and of engineers, groups of communications, sappers, radio and observation stations, ambulances, batteries, ovens, etc.

The Ceuta column was under the command of General Saro, and that of Melilla under General Fernández Pérez. Each one consisted of nine thousand men. With the Melilla brigade went Colonel Goded of the Military Staff, and Major Varela led the expeditionary forces. The first column of the Ceuta brigade was led by Colonel Franco, Commander of the Legion.

In successive orders the details of the operation were unfolding themselves, and the forces were informed with regard to their engagements immediately following their landing.

"No one is to stop to pick up the wounded except those designated for that purpose. . . . Those who land will immediately unload water and munitions. . . . It must always be kept in mind that the swift action of the officers upon landing, urging on their troops under enemy fire, will guarantee the success of the operation. . . . The officers may carry on the expedition a valise and a camp cot, but these articles are not to be unloaded on to the first barges. . . . Each individual soldier shall carry two days' rations of cold food and bread, ammunition, a canteen, four camp coats, sapper equipment, an individual medicine kit, an identification medal, pistols, and illumination and signal rockets."

Great care was taken that all the exigencies be attended to, but even so all the precautions seemed insufficient. A landing venture is always dangerous, and much more so when confronted by an embattled and numerous enemy (it was calculated that the Moors in arms numbered sixty thousand), emboldened by the retreat from Xauen, and with the advantage of a terrain which was equal to a fortress defending the shores.

In the orders given by General Sanjurjo who was in charge of the landing, and those of the commanders of the brigades, dictated during the days preceding the operation, the duties incumbent upon each soldier were precise and clear.

In the order of September 2 the objective was explained to General Saro's column, in which the skirmish forces under the command of Franco figured.

"At four o'clock in the morning the landing is to be made by surprise on the beach of Ixdain, and if it is successful an effort will be made to have the best troops surround the

enemy fortifications of Morro Nuevo, establishing there a
defensive front as extensive as possible. . . . The landed
forces will establish themselves as strongly as possible, especially those of General Saro. From the outset they will
establish an impregnable fortified base on the peninsula of
Morro Nuevo, which will be considered as the redoubt
against resistance and will permit the immediate accumula-
tion there of the greatest number of elements of all types."

On the third, fourth, and seventh of September, in various
orders of the commanding officers, it was ordered that the
Ceuta brigade be divided into three columns. The first was
to be called the "vanguard of the landing," and was to be
under the command of Colonel Franco. He was instructed
as follows:

"When the fleet is in front of the beach of Cebadilla, at
daybreak, by previous orders of Colonel Franco (carried out
in whatever manner is most convenient), the 'K' boats which
contain the units of the column and compose the first wave
of barges, carrying in advance and to the right of the line all
those vessels which transport the assault cars, shall go as
rapidly as possible to the beach of Ixdain to disembark their
human and material cargoes, making the landing with the
greatest possible speed and determination.

"While the forces are landing they are to go to the road
in spread-out sections and entrench themselves behind the
cars, maneuvering as Colonel Franco shall decide.

"The advance. The start of this phase will be announced
by Colonel Franco by such signals as he himself shall de-
termine, so that the land batteries, the fleet, and the air
forces will all be aware and ready as the firing and bombarding proceeds."

And at noon of the seventh, General Primo de Rivera,
general in command, dictated an order which stated, "The
commander of the column in the vanguard [Franco] has
absolute authority in the selection of land positions. He shall
mark out the front, and keep in mind that to cover the posi-

tions, and to carry out the necessary services and internal consolidation, he will need approximately twelve thousand men, with their corresponding cattle and materials."

And he added, "The operation and its general character being well understood, good will and initiative will counteract mistaken orders. But I want to insist that no place of landing can succeed nor be carried out except under the following conditions: first, by surprise, that is to say, not to carry it out at points especially aware, prepared, and defended; secondly, to maintain free from the firing the precise fringe of coast serving as a means of land communication and as a place for the landing of auxiliary forces."

In other words, the commander of the vanguard was entrusted with the selection of the place of landing, he was given full powers concerning all the immediate operations, and he was given complete authority for carrying out the operations of the advance.

On the afternoon of the seventh, the Spanish and French warships, and the vessels carrying the Ceuta brigade, made a demonstration in front of the beach of Suaní, to the east of Morro Nuevo. In previous days the squadrons had made demonstrations at various points off the coast of Gomara. The "K" motor barges, big-bellied and iron-clad, had landed the materials which corresponded to them. Each one was capable of holding three hundred men on foot. A sliding bridge would be thrown out in order to facilitate access to the shore.

At four o'clock in the afternoon the ships, an imposing fleet of eighty vessels, filed toward the bay of Alhucemas. "Quite a distance from the ships and close to the coast," writes a chronicler of the war, "traveled the merchant ship *Jaime II* carrying Colonel Franco, with the Legion embarked on the 'K' boats. The leader of the Legion studied at close range the landing beach, but when the vessel approached the rebel batteries of Morro, it was seen to change its course hastily, and speed up to escape their volleys, entering the line of the convoy. The quick maneuver and a noticeable firing distinct from the artillery of the squadron gave evidence that the rebels were responding to the cannon shots." On that trip Franco verified that which he had studied many times from the air on his many flights over Alhucemas.

That night the troops kept vigil in the Straits. The sky was clear and studded with sparkling little lights. There was a ripple on the water. The boats glided along like moving shadows in peaceful pleasure. The steep uneven edges of the African coast gave the appearance of a fantastic squadron, anchored and immovable.

All of a sudden, on the crests of the distant Riff mountains, the campfires blazed forth like red fountains, flaming trumpets that announced the impending war, and the sky was resplendent with a fiery bronze hue.

The advance column commanded by Colonel Franco consisted of the following forces: Banners Six and Seven, under the command of Lieutenant-Colonel Liniers, and a group of Tetuán Regulars under Lieutenant-Colonel Fiscer, *mejala* and Regulars from Larache under Major Villalba, and the expeditionary forces of Major Muñoz Grande and those of Captain Bescansa and Zabalza.

The restless sea had separated the ships of the convoy and they had to be brought together in formation. This was accomplished at eleven o'clock.

With the first light of daybreak there was activity on the ships, which were teeming with soldiers. The many clouds in the sky were ashen gray. At eight o'clock in the morning the bombardment began with a formidable and thunderous clatter. The one hundred and ninety cannons on the ships, thirty of high caliber, and the thirty-two pieces placed at Peñón roared. Land, air, and sea vibrated with the resounding clatter. From the ship *Dédalo* the hydroplanes took off while others arrived from the base at Mar Chica to sow with machine-gun bullets the lower part of Morro.

Africa, thus cursed and punished, trembled and creaked. Its very foundations were raised up in sudden volcanolike clouds of dust, in sudden fires, and in shattering quakes that scattered forth rocks and masses of branches.

At eleven forty the barges which constituted the first waves of the landing set out, towed and surrounded by other vessels. They were setting forth upon the great adventure. Their cannons were belching fire and whizzing out arches of destruction. These were clever barges, and in them went the Banners of the Legion, the expeditionary forces of Tetuán and Larache and fortification and engineering equipment. With the Legionnaires went Franco, their leader.

About a thousand meters distance from the coast the "K" boats were set loose. They carried the units of the advance column. And the barges, on their own, with the men under the protection of a curtain of steel, made their way to the beach of Ixdain in the face of the rather weak firing of enemy cannons, machine guns, and rifles. Checked by the hail of steel from the Spanish artillery, the adversary was listless.

Then the crucial moment arrived. The "K" boats were only fifty meters from shore. "The 'K' boats that carried the light assault cars," writes López Rienda, "were ordered to advance." But the bridges thrown out from the barges did not contact the land properly. A space remained which it was impossible for the cars to pass. At that moment Franco, that great leader of such admirable abilities, with the clear vision that he had on the field, saw that the fleeting moments were precious. And he did not hesitate to order the bugler to sound the signal to attack.

The forces hurled themselves into the water neck deep, holding their firearms in the air, the Legionnaires with Franco, Lieutenant-Colonel Liniers, and Majors Rada and

Verdú, and the expeditionary forces with their officers. Captain Rodríguez Bescansa was the first to reach land, and from there, turning toward those who were advancing, he cried, "Long live Spain!" "Long live Spain!" the soldiers answered by way of greeting, as they set foot on dry ground, their clothes clinging to their bodies and soaked with water, but with their guns held firmly in their hands.

Franco ordered the advance. The expeditionary forces marched along the left front and flank, while the Banners of the Legion made their way to the left to occupy the heights that dominated the beaches of Cebadilla and Los Frailes, "augmenting the front foreseen as a consequence of the displacement to the northeast." Early in the afternoon the Legionnaires dominated the heights, upon which they nailed their white standard, which bore a venerated named: "Valenzuela."

The landing was made at the price of one death, Lieutenant Hernández Menor, and five wounded. The guardians of Axdir who gathered to forestall the operation "were rapidly annihilated by the energy and mastery," says General Goded, "with which the landing was effected by the forces of Colonel Franco."

And from the same general came these words: "The front occupied by our troops followed the line of the heights facing the shores of Cebadilla, Ixdain, and Los Frailes, extending from the counterfronts of Mount Malmusi to the point of Morro Nuevo. It is a line admirably chosen, which is a credit to the tactical vision of Colonel Franco, and which by its natural strength and wise plan made it possible to hold back the furious attacks of the enemy on the following days."

In the selection of the landing place the studies and investigations of an illustrious naval officer, whose name cannot be overlooked when speaking of Alhucemas, were a contributing factor; namely, Carlos Boada, frigate captain.

The following days were tragic ones for the landed forces. The rough sea prevented the supplying of provisions regularly. Water was lacking and there was beginning to be a scarcity of munitions. The soldiers were inadequately sheltered. The only food consisted of sardines and hardtack. To these deficiencies and rigors must be added the furious attacks of the Riffs, who were endeavoring to drive the land forces into the sea. Goded's column suffered terrific night attacks.

It was not only the condition of the sea that complicated matters, there was another factor. Part of the forces of the Melilla column had to be taken posthaste to Tetuán to the rescue of the garrison at Kudia Tahar, which at the price of bloody sacrifices held back the avalanche unchained by Abd-el-Krim for the purpose of capturing Tetuán. On September 13 Kudia Tahar was liberated.

By the twentieth already fifteen thousand men had disembarked. An operation attempted by the expeditionary forces of Muñoz Grande and Varela resulted in two hundred casualties and five dead officers. The pressure of the enemy was becoming more and more dangerous, and it was necessary to go out and fight them off in order to hold them at bay.

Two days later began the advance to occupy Malmusis and Morro Viejo. Franco led the vanguard, with the plan to carry out the principal onslaught and the assault. Franco's troops met stiff resistance as they scaled the first heights of Malmusi Alto, producing among the expeditionary forces and the *mejala* a momentary hesitation which was valiantly overcome by the Sixth and Seventh Banners of the Legion led by Franco in person.

"There was a moment of confusion," writes a chronicler, referring to this critical juncture in the combat. "The first guerrillas of the expeditionary forces came upon a line along which mines had been planted. The explosions forced them to fall back. But Franco ordered two companies to advance to the attack of the first peak of Malmusi. Rapidly, with the

21st and 22nd companies, and Major Rada in command, the Legionnaires made their way to the first peak of the famous Cuernos de Xauen, which they soon captured."

From those peaks the Spanish soldiers dominated the whole panorama of Beni-Urriaguel. On Axdir the sword of Spain was raised avenged.

On September 30 another operation was carried out which had as its purpose the occupation of the Palomar and Adrar Seddun mountains, the boundaries which the troops were to establish as had been previously determined. The columns of Franco, Goded, and Vera intervened. Franco's men met the stiffest resistance at first, because of the land hazards and the strong concentration of the enemy there.

After some hard fighting the enemy was gradually driven from the heights, and in a supreme effort Franco's troops reached the top of the Palomar mountain. Its last defenders hurled themselves headlong over the cliffs. In this operation García Escámez, an officer of the Legion, and Varela, at the head of his expeditionary force, gained new laurels.

The road to Axdir was now open. On the second of October Franco's vanguard surrounded Mount Amekran and with the force of an impetuous flood the Spanish soldiers advanced upon the settlement which was the sinister haunt of Abd-el-Krim, the underground dungeon of Spanish prisoners, and the gangrenous center from which rebellion radiated over all Morocco. Flames erased and purified that oracular name.

Spain was triumphant. The conqueror's heel had crushed the heart of the rebellion. Abd-el-Krim was a fugitive. At noon Generals Primo de Rivera and Sanjurjo arrived at Axdir. "This day," says one of the notes of the Marquis de Estella, "has been a day of great moment." The various beaches of Alhucemas were filled with soldiers bathing.

The island, captive a short while before and abandoned, was now teeming with traffic as it was being salvaged by boats carrying things to the shore. The encampments were quiet. In short, the Spanish troops were in complete control, the prize of a hard-fought struggle.

With the operation of the 13th on Mount Xixafea the operations of the landed forces were considered completed, and some, carried away with optimism, were convinced that the war in Africa was over. But that was not the case. Winter delayed the campaigns which were resumed in the spring of 1926. During that year and the first half of 1927 Morocco was conquered under intelligent direction in which the efforts of Goded, Mola, Castro Girona, Varela, Balmes, González Carrasco, Capaz, Dolla, Sanz de Larín, and other officers under the authority of Sanjurjo were outstanding. On July 10, 1927, the general in command made the following proclamation to his troops, in which are written with truth these historic words:

"As a result of today's movements the last remains of the rebellion have been crushed, we have occupied all of our zone of the protectorate, and the campaign in Morocco, which has constituted a problem for the government for the past eighteen years, is now ended.

"The landing at Alhucemas in September of 1925, where for the first time the solution to this problem was confronted bravely and with determination, and from whence the rebellion was attacked at its root, created the base of operations which made possible the rapid and decisive unfolding of the campaign which, begun on May 8, 1926, and continued methodically even during the winter, made it possible for us to end the rebellion in fifteen months of continuous and rigorous operations. And so today, this army, Spain's army, may say that it has put the word 'end' to a problem perhaps the most dangerous that has confronted the nation in recent years."

Primo de Rivera asked for recompense, "not only to do justice, but to exalt day by day, if it was still possible, the military spirit." Franco figured among the promotions granted for merit gained in the Alhucemas campaign, being raised to the rank of general. He was thirty-two years of age. He was conferred the second Military Medal, and made Knight Commander of the Legion of Honor and granted the badge of Military and Naval Merit by France.

CHAPTER XIII

Unscathed and Unbowed

AFTER fourteen long years of active military life almost uninterrupted Franco returned to the Peninsula. He returned unscathed and unbowed.

He had participated in the operations of Beni-Arós, the reconquest of Melilla, the retreat from Xauen, and the landing at Alhucemas, always in the vanguard as leader of forces in combat. The records of the war are full of references to the bravery of Franco. Bullets seemed to revere him as they did the prophets of Moorish legend who had miraculous powers and turned bullets into rose petals. Through the course of the African campaigns the path was covered with graves, and many commanders and officers had fallen.

Millán Astray was wounded while speaking with Franco. Franco had seen two of his aides-de-camp and his standard-bearer fall dead at his feet. González Tablas, Valenzuela, Fontanes, Serrano Orive, Temprano, Arredondo, and many others had died. Of the officers of the First Banner, which Franco commanded, not ten per cent survived. He had bullet-riddled caps and cloaks, various horses he was riding had been wounded, and at Alhucemas the explosion of a shell buried him. But all these warnings neither terrified him nor separated him from the danger zone to which he was again to return with his unshakable calmness.

The only time that Millán Astray admonished him was for the fearlessness with which he defied gunfire in the advances. Sanjurjo jokingly threatened to club him if he should find him again on his white horse in the thick of the firing line. The corporal in the Legion, and author, Carlos Micó, convalescing in Madrid in 1922, met Franco when he was passing through the city. The Commander of the Legion was on his way to visit his mother and his fiancée. "I look at you," he said, "with surprise and astonishment on seeing that you are unscathed. I have always seen you in horrifying danger, and always without care, so that not believing you to be unconscious I am obliged to believe the occultists when they say that some extraordinary power drives bullets away from your path."

Franco could say with pride, "I have seen death at my side many a time, but thanks to my good fortune, it has not known me. . . ."

But it was not all luck. Franco's was the fortune that accompanies great leaders, and which is in great part the result of his own perspicacity and talent. Franco had learned the art of war. And he did not hide the secret, but revealed it. He saw that the Moors criticized the majority of the officers who arrived in Morocco for "not knowing how" to fight. By this they meant that they lacked the martial spirit, and that they limited themselves to the rigid application of rules without modifying them to meet the special characteristics of African warfare.

War in Morocco was full of surprises, and Franco, so unconcerned in outward appearance, was ever watchful. In this school of watchfulness he taught his Legionnaires, and as a result he, one who hated to lose lives, saved an infinite number of casualties. The soldiers knew it, were grateful to him, and admired him. Franco knew the cleverness of the enemy, and that the latter made use not only of his rifle but of another powerful weapon, the terrain. That weapon he recommended to his troops constantly, and he taught them to "climb the slopes with precaution, and on all fours to the last step when necessary, always ready to meet the enemy and avoid being taken by surprise." "The division shall never form in rigid order." "The enemy never gets to his steel weapon except when the soldiers run." For fighting on the hills and slopes he recommended a practice contrary to the orthodox precepts. And finally, he knew that nothing disconcerted the enemy more than serenity. In battle the man who remained master of himself always held a decisive superiority over his adversary. And against panic and sudden terror, which sometimes appeared among the troops, bringing disasters such as the one at Annual, there was no remedy other than good officers, determined and unimpressionable, who stuck to their posts.

Franco mastered the science and art of war. A million men fitted in his head was the expression of a famous military critic. Millán Astray said that he was the prototype of the soldier who reacts to a situation with intelligence and energy. He would obtain minute information concerning the conditions of the battleground and he would anticipate with precision that which might happen and rapidly work out a solution for each particular case. He always knew the extent of his resources and the potentialities of the men at his command. And to these exceptional qualities he united bravery.

As a result he has been able to master critical situations which have presented themselves before him with risk of disaster, and has turned them to victories. That is what took place at Gurugú, and at the Palomas mountains where an enemy that was enraged and superior in numbers attempted to surround Franco's forces, a maneuver which lacked strategy. "That which creates victory is, above all, the action of the commanding officer," said Marshal Foch.

In the many tests he was put to in the course of his campaigns, Franco came out not only unbowed but triumphant. General Sanjurjo commented that "Franquito," as he affectionately called him, never failed in an enterprise which he ordered and he always accomplished that which he was ordered to do, regardless of how great the obstacles might be, no matter how bold an effort was necessary, and no matter how difficult the undertaking.

His was a vocation entirely to his fancy. He had a will that was accustomed and invulnerable to eclipses or misfortunes, a temperament acclimated to war, and an intense patriotism.

On campaign Franco was never idle, not even on the monotonous days of inactivity which invited rest and pleasure in the refuge of the encampment or in the casino of the city. He would spend the time watching from the ramparts with the aid of his binoculars. Whenever possible he would ride out on horseback to study the terrain. He would make rough drafts and put to memory even the most minute topographical detail which might be useful at the hour of battle.

To this rigorous preparation must be attributed in great part his military success. When he started a march he knew exactly where he was going and where he must be cautious. He knew the topographical conditions for defense and offense. The soldiers followed him blindly because that study made by the officer in command had been made for the sake of all of them.

This is the source of the fame which surrounds him as a saver of lives and a lucky soldier. The operations directed by him were carried out with a minimum of casualties. Franco knew that the secret of retaining the loyalty of his soldiers was in their knowing that they were well officered and that their leader valued the lives of his men as much as he valued his own life.

During nearly all of the African campaigns Spain was indifferent. An indifference which at times was converted into open opposition. The war in Morocco was never popular. It started when the country was still convalescing from its grave colonial problems. But the forces of revolution took advantage of that to discredit the army and other institutions, and to incite the people, making more wearisome and more costly a problem which a less disorganized and less agitated nation would have resolved without the catastrophes, hecatombs, crises, and insurrections that Spain suffered.

In the early part of the year 1921 a phase of this propaganda against the war in Morocco was the opposition to raises in military rank for merit in active service, upheld in great part by a few officers whose career consisted in their being listed in the military register. The subject was discussed in a professional journal which advocated the formation of a body of colonial officers beside those of the Peninsular Army. Franco, in Xauen, wrote an article which he sent to the review, but it was not published because it contained ideas which were foreign to the opinion of the editor. The article was entitled, "The Merit of Active Service," and the following paragraphs are copied from it:

". . . My desire is only to present on this occasion the danger to the Army and military activities which lies in attempting to solve these problems at a distance, without knowing how to weigh in the balance of justice the hardships and sufferings of a thankless campaign, and the great number of officers who die gloriously for their country, increasing by their actions the fame of the infantry. They are the men who uphold the honor of the nation!

"The military problem of Morocco is, in general, the work of the infantry. They form the nucleus of the army, and with the cavalrymen, in a proportional number, they fill the ranks of the front-line troops. It is the infantry who, on the icy and stormy nights, keep vigil over the sleeping encampments, scale under fire the highest peaks, and fight and die without obtaining a just reward for their voluntary sacrifice and heroism.

"In the recent operations the painful casualties speak with greater eloquence than what can be said in these lines.

There died captains and lieutenants of the glorious Regulars, enthusiastic officers who had served several years on campaign with these troops, carried on by their great military enthusiasm and the hope of some day achieving a just reward for their sacrifice.

"This reward is the point about which articles and projects revolve. And some speak of a body of colonial officers, as though the future of our protectorate were the maintenance of a large army here, and also believing that the officer who works with enthusiasm and specializes in the problems of this war would be willing to renounce forever his place in the Peninsular Army.

"The African campaign is the best practical school, if not the only one, for our army. In it are weighed definite values and merits, and the officers of high attainment in Africa will some day be the body and soul of the Peninsular Army. But in order not to destroy that enthusiasm, and not to kill that spirit, which we should value as a precious jewel, it is necessary and indispensable to grant a just reward for merit in war. Otherwise that stimulus would be lost which guards over those ambitions which otherwise would be smothered to death by the weight of a military register in the idle life at the garrisons.

"As for our activities in Africa no one can deny that to permit those ideas would be a death blow to the spirit of our shock troops, which if formerly they had numerous aspirants to figure in their number, now are unable to replace their bloody casualties, for the destiny of the infantryman is only that glorious death which little by little is taking the toll of those that are still here.

"Let the infantrymen, therefore, measure their steps, let them turn their eyes to these Moroccan fields, let them fix their attention upon these modest cemeteries which cover the remains of so many glorious infantrymen, and they will not fail to see the necessity, with regard to the infantry, for them to unite in a tight embrace so that without unjust haggling the just and desired reward be granted for merit in battle."

This article was contained in a book published by Franco in 1922. It is entitled *Marruecos. Diario de una Bandera.* In it he relates in great detail the story of the Legion on to the battles of the campaign to reconquer Melilla, in which the First Banner under Franco's command participated so actively. That same Legion which he trained for the war in Uad Lau, and with which he landed to rescue Melilla.

He relates in the book his impressions of those agitated and burning months, shaken by a heroic storm during which the Legion was the implacable battering ram of the Moor, and an army famous and exemplary through its courage and bravery. It is the record book of a leader who follows with exactness and punctuality the experiences of the Legion, and it is also a showcase in which the author preserves with great care and respect the proofs of the heroism of his men, and a second file in which are recorded and preserved the warlike virtues of those who show valor with the disregard of Roman gladiators.

Franco had departed from Morocco, but his name was to be incorporated for all time in that chapter of Spanish history. He was one of its outstanding figures, both in the conquest and in the reconquest. His participation in the landing at Alhucemas is not brought out in full detail and with its full importance in the official records, even though the work and responsibility of the Commander of the Legion are given credit in expressive and eloquent words. A great part of that work of Franco's in the landing as well as in other Moroccan enterprises has been anonymously recorded, which is in keeping with his character and the exigencies of his simplicity and modesty. Franco does not cater to popularity. During the Melilla campaign of 1921, when the newspaper reporters were hovering around in search of news and unusual incidents there was not a Legionnaire, officer, or friendly Moor who escaped the siege of interviewers, but Franco was inaccessible to the avidity of the newspaper correspondents.

It remains to be said that Franco was one of those who drew up the plan for the landing at Alhucemas, and that General Primo de Rivera gave special weight to his advice when he decided to carry out the plan. But Franco was not satisfied with being only the theorist who made the plans, but instead, once the plan was approved, he assumed the responsibility of carrying it out in practice, like those composers of musical scores who at the hour of performance hold the baton and direct the orchestra, so as not to evade any responsibility or impose upon others faults that may be their own. And because Franco had the plans and details of the operation all worked out in his head, he was able to make changes freely and on short notice to which Goded attributes in great part the success of the enterprise.

The Marquis of Estella also utilized the services of Franco in his negotiations for the purpose of obtaining an understanding with the French army. Marshal Lyautey knew the Commander of the Legion personally. The marshal, as he well demonstrated, was a man who had the ability to read into the future of soldiers. He said that Franco was one of the most promising soldiers of our time. A few years after this prophecy Franco was successfully launching the reconquest of half of Spain!

CHAPTER XIV

The General Military Academy

A DECREE of the Dictatorship restored the General Military Academy, renowned in military history, in which the cadets of the army were to enroll for two years of preparatory studies before entering the special military academies, such as those for infantry, cavalry, artillery, engineering, and commissariat. The purpose was to create a real intimate solidarity among all the branches of the army.

Franco was named Director of the Academy, but not without resistance, considering the fact that there were other names more prominent than his to choose from for the position. Franco was the youngest general in Spain and in all Europe.

When Franco arrived at Zaragoza, he immediately realized that he had to found the Academy whose direction had been entrusted to him. Everything was yet to be done, from the setting up of buildings in which to lodge the cadets, to the drawing up of entrance examinations. The Academy, at the beginning of the year 1928, was only on paper, a decree published in the *Gaceta*. But Franco, from the moment of his appointment, prepared himself for the post to which he had been entrusted. He studied, he took the advice of technical experts, and later he was to visit the military schools of Berlin and Dresden to copy from them that which they offered which was most exemplary and modern.

Once in Zaragoza he called together the faculty of the

Academy in one of the rooms of the Carmen Barracks, and surprised those gathered with the statement, "We will hold the convocation in June, and the course will begin in October."

The members of the faculty looked at each other and smiled. That optimism of the director seemed to them to be mere bravado. In October! Where? How? Everything is lacking! But it took only a few days for the skeptics to rectify their ideas and realize that the man who presided over them was capable of fulfilling what he promised. Meetings followed. Through Franco's office filed architects, contractors, builders, and military men. He wrote letters. He worked day and night. He met with the various professors to draw up the examinations. In the camp of San Gregorio the buildings were being built. One day the convocation for the entrance examinations in June was published, and on the date planned the convocation was held in one of the rooms of the Costa Building, with all the faculty in attendance.

At the completion of the examinations, there was again uncertainty. When would the courses begin? Franco answered, "In October, and in the proper building of the Academy."

And in order to bind himself further by his decision he designated October 3 for the entrance of the two hundred and fifteen, out of seven hundred and eighty-five applicants, who passed the examination.

On the first day of that month the buildings which constituted the barracks were taken over, for the Academy building was still under construction, and in twenty-four hours the premises were prepared to receive the cadets. On the 5th of October classes began. There was a simple military demonstration, the first manifestation of discipline and enthusiasm on the part of the cadets, celebrated in one of the courts of the barracks, in the presence of General Primo de Rivera, the presiding officer of the government, who wished to attend the inauguration of a work in which he had placed great hope.

General Franco made his first speech as Director of the Academy:

"Gentlemen cadets, today soldiers of our army, and army officers of the future, we welcome you to this academy, in which you will begin your military career, and where you will receive the teachings of this brilliant group of officers of our army, which, united in a common bond of love for Spain and fidelity to the King, anxiously awaited the moment when it would receive you and stamp upon your character the elevated spirit of the Spanish soldiery. In them you will find a constant guide, and an edifying example, for it is not in vain that they treasure the purest and most spotless virtues. To the experience of those who, aged in the profession of arms, have dedicated their lives to work and study, will be united that of those others who, more fortunate in war, could contrast their skill and enthusiasm, and who today cover their breasts with the most esteemed military decorations.

"And destiny willed that on this day of your admission as cadets, a day so happy to us, we should be honored by having the inauguration of the course presided over by the presiding officer of the government, General Primo de Rivera, the Minister of War, the Director General of Instruction, the civil and military authorities of this city, and a brilliant array of the veteran officials of the garrison, those who tomorrow, continuing our work, will be your teachers, and at whose side you will contrast your virtues and knowledge. And then you will transfuse into the old standing regiments the new sap of the fieriness and enthusiasm of your youth and the sane optimism of your lofty hopes.

"It is not a new center of learning which opens its doors to you today, for it has a most ancient lineage in the annals of our military history. It began in the beginning of the past century. It was in 1809 that the first military

academy of a general character for various divisions of
the Army came into existence, due to the energy of a famous
artilleryman, Lieutenant-Colonel Don Marino Gil de
Bernabé, who in the midst of the vicissitudes of war gave
life to that academy established in Seville based upon the
Battalion of Honor of the Toledo students.

"That splendid school existed for fourteen years, for a
time in camp tents, and for a time in old monasteries, it
passed from Seville to Cádiz, from Cádiz to San Carlos,
and from there, after having the honor of fighting at
Puente Zuazo, the last bulwark of our independence, it
went to the Alpujarras, where it was dissolved. But its
memory was kept alive, and it was born again in the year
1824. By that time, over a century ago, it was recognized
to be a necessity that the youths who dedicate themselves
to the career of arms should be educated in the same
principles and under the same roof, as was stated in the
official resolution that created it.

"It was the unfortunate life of the past century, with its
domestic campaigns, which carried the General Military
College from Segovia to Madrid, and from there to Toledo,
where under the direction of the Count de Clonard it
attained the renown due it, until 1850, when after twenty-
five years of existence and of giving to the Fatherland the
most outstanding generals of the past century, again
domestic partisanships led to its dissolution.

"Thirty-two years of absence were not sufficient to
obscure its memory, and on February 20, 1882, His
Majesty the King, Don Alfonso XIII, in compliance with
the wishes of the Army, created the General Military
Academy.

"Brilliant and unforgettable was the story of this center
for those who filled its ranks, many of whom stand out
today at the top of the military roll of the Army. Among
the memories of its brilliant professors that of its first
director, Don José Galvis, and that of the exemplary dean

of studies, Don Federico Vázquez Landa, stood out, just as the name of General Primo de Rivera, who is honoring us with his presence at this moment, is held in high esteem by the cadets today.

"I have summarized here in a few words the history which you are destined to continue and of which you should feel proud.

"Imitate the virtues of those who preceded you in this dignity, which are contained in the Decalogue of the Cadet. Guard this as a precious relic and take care of it with the purest love, and I am sure that you will emulate the history of those loyal soldiers, valiant and sacrificing gentlemen, who for over a century wrote the most brilliant pages in the history of our nation. It is a history that repeats itself. It is the wise orders of Charles III, which never grow antiquated, the nobility of those hidalgos which again dwells in our hearts, and the unconquered and heroic city of Zaragoza which set the scene, offering to you in their stones and monuments the first and most solid lesson of heroic sacrifices.

"The military life is not a road to pleasure and delight. As we have shown, it carries with it great sufferings, hardships, and sacrifices. Glory also, but like the rose it comes forth among thorns.

"It must not be forgotten that he who suffers conquers, and that daily resisting and conquering is the school of triumph, and is the road to the heroism of tomorrow. And as proof of your enthusiasm, of your future voluntary sacrifices, of your discipline, of the unflinching fidelity to our King, and of your desire for the greatness of the Fatherland, cry out with me: Long live Spain! Long live the King! Long live the Army!"

General Primo de Rivera brought the affair to a close with a few haranguing words exalting the work of the soldier, and evoking past glories which touched the emotions, for in that courtyard, before his eyes, were two cadets who carried his surname, the sons of his brother Fernando, who died at Monte Arruit, and who were to be executed in the great upheaval of 1936.

The course had begun. The life of the Academy reflected the seriousness which its director stamped on all of its activities; namely, formality in personal conduct, stern military training, and rigorous discipline, which were unalterable.

The Decalogue of the Cadet ordered:

1. To have a great love of country and fidelity to the King, made manifest in every act of one's life.

2. To have military enthusiasm, reflected in one's vocation and discipline.

3. To unite to one's honorable behavior constant concern for his reputation.

4. To be faithful in the fulfillment of obligations, and prompt in service.

5. Never to complain, nor tolerate it.

6. To be liked by subordinates and sought by superiors.

7. To be ready for any sacrifice, seeking and desiring always to be employed in the occasions of greatest risk and fatigue.

8. To have a sense of noble companionship, sacrificing for one's comrade, and taking joy in his success, rewards, and progress.

9. To have a love for responsibility, and decision in solving problems.

10. To be brave and self-sacrificing.

The textbooks were suppressed, and replaced by official regulations and explanations and lectures of the faculty, from which a reference text, or abstract, was distributed among the students.

General Franco supervised and attended to everything, from the rectification of an unclear question on the questionnaire to the expense for supporting the cadets so that the cookery budget would not be unbalanced.

Franco, in love with the Academy, was wedded to his work. He observed vigilantly the latest practices and teachings that were adopted by the leading academies of Europe, in order to adopt them at Zaragoza. But above that which he could import was the contribution of his own ability, experience, intuition, and genius, which was, in the last analysis, what gave splendor to the Academy and was the driving force as it developed under a halo of fame and renown.

The first oath of allegiance to the flag, the old one that belonged to the old General Academy, was celebrated on June 5, 1930, in the courtyard of María Cristina. The King and General Berenguer, who was at the head of the government, were present. Mass was said, and at the close of the ceremonies General Iborra presented the flag to the King, who placed it in the hands of General Franco.

"Sir," he said, "it has been forty-three years since the General Military Academy received from your august Mother, Queen María Cristina, of lasting memory, this precious flag. It received it with love and affection, and this precious flag was the banner of that institution, which always was noted for its discipline. On this banner are stamped the four cardinal virtues, constituting an emblem of self-abnegation. The new cadets of this General Military Academy will be able to fulfill well their oaths. It is thus that we have taught them. We know that this flag represents the King, the Constitution, and our Country.

"You, gentlemen cadets, bear in mind that that red color is even redder because it has been watered with the blood of various generations of soldiers. That the gold represents the glory of Spain and the monarchy. And now, render the honors. Prepare arms! Aim! Fire!"

A few final words from the King concerning military solidarity, and the four hundred and ninety-four students took an oath of allegiance to the flag.

The precision and rhythm with which the cadets maneuvered produced surprise.

"We have never seen anything like it," assured the King on congratulating General Franco for that extraordinarily beautiful and martial spectacle. He invited the battalion of cadets to go to Madrid to serve as Palace guard.

On the occasion of the death of the Queen Mother, General Franco published the following extraordinary order:

"Gentlemen cadets, the death today of Her Royal Majesty the Queen Doña María Cristina, constitutes a day of mourning for the nation and of grieving for all good Spaniards.

"The attachment of the Spanish people and her army to so august a Queen is so great, that fitting words fail me in this moment of sentiment and sorrow.

"Since the year 1879, when by her marriage to Don Alfonso XII she assumed the Spanish crown, her person presided over the most important events of the life of our nation, and it was upon the death of her august husband in the year 1885 when, with the regency, she placed upon her shoulders the heavy burden of governing Spain. She lived and suffered with it, having the most violent tempests to subdue, in which to the preoccupations of the destiny of the nation, she united that of the care and education of the child King, to whom she turned over the crown in May of 1902 after seventeen years of regency. And following the solemn act of investiture, our King, with the applause of the people, decreed the honors of Queen which she was to have during her lifetime.

"There is not a single episode in the history of her reign in which she does not share the sorrow or happiness of her people, and it did not know a need or misfortune that was not attended to by her charitable hand, and if the nation owes her gratitude for her sacrifices and kindnesses, what does not the army owe to her, the object of her vigilance! . . .

"How many wounded officers and soldiers, upon awakening in their hours of fever, saw seated at their side our august Queen! How many others felt on their wounded bodies the balm of her royal hands! And how many mothers did not experience the deep emotion of feeling that the Queen was taking their place at the head of the bed of their sons! . . .

"Her memory will never be forgotten by those of us who lived in her reign, and we will concentrate more our affection upon her august son, His Majesty the King, and the royal family, if that is possible, holding always as our norm that fidelity is the most precious quality of the gentleman, and that it should always reign in the heart of the good soldier.

"Long live Spain! Long live the King!

Your General Director,
Francisco Franco"

On the 8th of October, 1930, the Prince of Asturias visited the Academy. On the occasion of the prince's visit General Franco saw an excellent opportunity to end in a cordial manner an old dispute in Spain which appeared in Zaragoza, the hostility between the cadets and the university students, which was endemic in the cities where both were present. The rivalry also existed in the Aragonese capital, and Franco was determined to put an end to it. Recently an incident had created a state of excitement among the cadets and the university students, whose strained relations threatened to break with a crash. The visit of the prince offered the opportunity that Franco was looking for. It was the occasion of the banquet held in the dining room of the Academy in honor of His Highness. The general sent to the rector of the University, Señor Rocasolano, a number of invitations for the students, and these were

placed at the head of each of the tables occupied by the
cadets. The friendly gesture softened the university students, and from that day the rivalry was converted into
a friendly relationship. The students paid back the cadets
with a dinner at which the places of honor were for the
students of the Academy.

Arms and letters joined hands and lived happily.

Also in this month of October, 1930, the Academy
received a visit that will be memorable, that of the French
Minister of War, Maginot, accompanied by the Spanish
ambassador to Paris, Señor Quiñones de León, and the
French General George.

Maginot, the man to whom France owes its best defense
of today, the sagacious driving power behind the armed
forces of his country, did not hide his surprise at what he
saw. In his eulogy, he said that it was without question
the outstanding center of military training in Europe. And
when he returned to his country he repeated the praises
to the press, and the General Military Academy acquired
considerable fame and name.

The Minister of War decorated Franco with the insignia
of Commander in the Legion of Honor, and, at the banquet
honoring Maginot, the Director of the Academy rendered
homage to the man who "renounced his political career
and sacrificed all at the outbreak of the Great War, in
order to place himself at the service of his nation as a simple
soldier."

"Of how you served your country on the front," added
Franco, "your history and honorable wounds give answer.
All in all, to the satisfaction of receiving the minister of
a friendly nation, is added something very dear to us, that
of a French comrade, of that glorious army which in the
Moroccan campaign we learned to know and admire while
fighting together for the cause of civilization and progress."

A minister like Maginot, who was profoundly interested
in military questions, could not make a mere formal visit

to an Academy in which he found so many details and so many exemplary teachings. He informed himself of the methods which were being pursued, of the studies which composed the course, and the method by which the faculty had been selected. He then knew that the majority of the professors had fought in Africa and that the least any of them had served in action was five years. Maginot then summarized his impressions by saying, "with an army commanded by these future officers you can go anywhere."

In November, 1930, General Franco attended the course for generals and colonels which was held at Versailles, as preparation for the high command. Tactical problems on maps, movements of troops on the field, and questions of strategy were studied. In one of the sessions there was a discussion. Franco spoke up and before a blackboard he began to develop his ideas. Voices were stilled and silence reigned. Generals and colonels drew up around Franco, and the gathering of that day was converted into a lesson which the Spanish general taught to the strategists of all the nations gathered at Versailles, who listened, absorbed with admiration, to the youngest general of Europe.

CHAPTER XV

The Republic

SOME municipal elections — an unusual event — caused Spain, which had slept as a Monarchy, to awaken on April 14, 1931, with a Liberty Cap.

The Republicans themselves were the first to be surprised by that triumph that overran the streets, which entered their homes like a cyclone. And at the smell of that triumph Republicans appeared with the astonishing multiplicity of a contagion. Few resisted that influence which invaded all quarters. Whoever had any connection with the government made every effort to ingratiate himself as much as possible with the new regime with an excessive and gushing loyalty.

The day after the Republic had been established General Franco made known the event to the General Academy with an order which is a model of sobriety and decorum:

"A Republic having been proclaimed in Spain, the highest powers of the state being assumed by the provisional government, it behooves us all at this moment to co-operate with discipline and the solid virtues so that peace may reign and the nation may adjust itself through the natural legal channels.

"If at all times discipline and the exact fulfillment of duty have reigned in this military center, they are even more necessary today when the army needs, serene and united, to sacrifice all personal opinion and ideology for the good of the nation and the peaceful tranquillity of the Fatherland."

Two days later, it was rumored in Madrid that the

Republican government was going to transfer Franco to the high command of Spain in Morocco, and one paper printed a photograph of the general and confirmed the rumor. Franco rectified this in a letter dated April 18 which was written to the editor of *ABC,* in which he said "that neither the provisional government could have thought of such a thing, nor would I accept any renounced post which might be interpreted as anterior complaisance on my part with the regime recently inaugurated, or as a consequence of having been able to have the least lukewarmness or reserve in the fulfillment of my obligations or in the loyalty which I owed and held toward those who until yesterday represented the nation in the monarchical regime. On the other hand, it is my firm purpose to respect and revere, as always, the national sovereignty, and it is my desire that this power be expressed through its adequate juridical channels."

These and other events meant that from that time forward those who suffered from the sudden congestion of Republicanism that circumstances created, accused Franco of lukewarmness toward the regime, and ended by marking him out as a hostile element. From the boiling turbulence of the first days, Spain passed into a world of fantasy, where fingers beckoned to those seeking shelter and where on every street corner men with concealed faces plotted against the Republic. Stoolpigeons and spies were in their glory, and soon the General Military Academy was denounced as a dangerous monarchical center.

To a Minister of War of the stamp of Azaña, who surrounded his politics with a crushing machine, no better gift could have been offered him than the suppression, destruction, and pulverization of a military work or institution. And so he ordered that along with its course of studies the General Academy at Zaragoza be closed. He suppressed it with a stroke of the pen.

Franco learned of the suppression through the press, for at the time he was at the annual maneuvers of the Academy in the Pyrenees. He refused to believe it. Could it be possible that for pure partisan satisfaction a work that guaranteed for the Spanish Army an ideal staff could be undone, a work that would be the mind and backbone of the nation's strength? What kind of a regime was that which did not permit what was essential for the solidity and permanence of the nation?

On July 14, General Franco bade farewell to the cadets with a stirring speech, as an extraordinary order of the Academy, which caused a sensation all over Spain.

"Gentlemen cadets, I would like to perform this act of departure with the solemnity of past years, when, to the tune of the National Anthem, we would take out our flag for the last time, and as yesterday, you would kiss its rich folds, a chill of emotion running through your bodies, and your eyes beclouded at the thought of the glories it embodies. But the lack of an official flag limits our affair to these unfortunate moments when, on making you the object to which our farewell is directed, I wish to give you as a lesson in military morality these last words of advice.

"The General Military Academy has functioned for three years, and now its resplendent sun is about to rest. Years through which we lived by your side, educating and instructing you, and attempting to forge for Spain the most competent and honorable staff of officers that any nation could hope to possess.

"We had real satisfaction on that road of thorns when the most capable foreign experts lavished warm eulogies upon our work, studying and praising our system and setting it up as a model among modern institutions of military training. Real satisfaction which we offer to Spain for we are proud of our work and convinced of its greatest possible success.

"We studied our army, its faults and its virtues, and correcting the former, we have increased the latter while noting a real evolution in procedures and systems. Thus we saw rigid and out-of-date textbooks succumb before the pressure of a modern faculty, conscious of its mission and at odds with such bastard interests.

"Hazing, an ancient and vicious custom of military academies and barracks, was unknown due to your understanding and nobleness.

"Venereal diseases, to which our youth has hitherto succumbed, did not make their appearance here, thanks to our watchfulness and to an adequate preventive action.

"Physical culture and daily exercises in the open air have helped in your military training, and have given you athletic bodies, which insure that there will be no weedy and rickety specimens in military circles. The entrance examinations, automatic and anonymous, previously open to intrigue and influence, were not degenerated by recommendation and favor, and today you can pride yourselves in your progress and need not blush at the old and antiquated methods of an earlier day.

"A profound revolution has taken place in military training, which previously had forced upon it the corollary of intrigue and passion on the part of those who profited in preserving such pernicious methods.

"Our Decalogue of the Cadet selected from our wise ordinances the best and most pure, and was offered as an indispensable creed which would take firm hold on your lives; and in these times when gentlemanliness and honor suffer constant rebuke, we have succeeded in making good our pride in being gentlemen, maintaining among you a high spirituality.

"Through it, in these moments when reforms and new military changes close the doors of this place, we must rise to the occasion, controlling our internal sorrow at the disappearance of our work, thinking only altruistically. The machine is in pieces, but the work lives on. You are our work, the seven hundred and twenty officers who tomorrow will be in company with the common soldier, whom you will guard and lead; who, constituting a great portion of the professional army, will be, without doubt, champions of loyalty, gentlemanliness, discipline, the fulfillment of duty and the spirit of sacrifice for country, all qualities inherent in the true soldier, among which stands out above all discipline, that sublime virtue indispensable to the life of any army, and which you are obligated to keep as the most precious of your possessions.

"Discipline! . . . never well defined and understood. Discipline! . . . which carries with it no merit when the command is pleasant and easy. Discipline! . . . which shows its true worth when the mind advises otherwise, when the heart fights to rise up in spiritual rebellion, or when the command is arbitrary or erroneous. This is the discipline which we inculcate in you. This is the example which we offer you.

"Elevate your thoughts toward the Fatherland, and sacrifice all for it, for if there is choice and free will for the common citizen, that is not so for those who receive the sacred care of the arms of the nation, and who for its service must sacrifice all their actions.

"I hope that this companionship born in these first days of your military life, spent together, will last through the years, and that our love for our adopted arms will always have as its aim the welfare of the nation and consideration and mutual affection among the members of the Army. Fellowship that carries with it help to the comrade in distress, happiness in his progress, applause for the one who stands out, and sympathy for the one who has been misguided or lost, for your generosity must be steeped in the high concept of honor, and in this way you will prevent those who from day to day were guilty of abusing the benevolence of their companions, which is complicity, from being met tomorrow by some unforeseen calamity and becoming a pernicious example of immorality and injustice in the Army.

"The concept of honor is not exclusive to a regiment, troop, or corps, but is the patrimony of the Army, and is subject to the traditional rules of gentlemanliness and nobility. He who believes himself watchful of the good name of his corps by turning over to another corps what would redound little to the glory of his own, offends gravely.

"A matter, this, which even though repeated many times, I should not silence, since there is no longer a tomorrow for me to counsel you.

"I cannot say to you, as before, that you leave here your home, for after today it will have disappeared. But I can assure you that, scattered throughout Spain, you will carry this place in your hearts, and that in your future we place our hopes and expectations. That when in the course of time your temples become gray, and your competence makes you masters in your profession, you will appreciate the magnitude and worth of our efforts. Then your memory and sound judgment will be our most precious recompense.

"We feel today, as we bid farewell, the satisfaction of a duty fulfilled, and we unite our sentiments and vehement desires for the greatness of our nation crying out united: Long live Spain!"

This speech displeased the government deeply, and Azaña officially warned the Director of the Military Academy.

The lacerating effect of the speech was still fresh when Franco, now ready, presented himself, as was his duty, to the minister. The latter said to him, "I have re-read your extraordinary order to the students and I must believe that you didn't realize what you wrote."

"Mr. Minister," answered the general, "I write nothing which I have not thought over previously."

"Yes, I had thought it out, and if I had to write it over again," he told his friends, "I wouldn't even change a comma."

In the speech was summarized the work of the Academy, that which had been done and that which was promised for the near future. All remained crushed and destroyed by the fury of politics. Franco saw undone the work which he had undertaken heart and soul, with all his military enthusiasm and zealous patriotism.

But this was not alone what had inspired him to make that speech, which was a lamentation and a warning, a protest and a watchword. For he saw the darkening horizon of Spain, and a society that was being decomposed by gangrenous politics whose corrupting action was rapid and fatal. And his cry asking for discipline "when the heart fights to rise up in spiritual rebellion, or when the command is arbitrary or erroneous" reflected the tremendous effort necessary to hold back the impetus with which he fought to give full reign to his indignation, to end a policy which to him had as its postulates injustice and ignominy.

The dissolution was followed by cruelty. Azaña did not consider his fierce rancor satisfied if he did not flourish his orders with traces of cruelty.

The Academy, which had cost many millions to endow with the most perfect equipment, laboratories, instruments and machinery for study, and fields for maneuvers and sports, was transformed into barracks. In a few months there was not to remain even a memory of what had been a leading center of military training in Europe and of the world.

For almost a year General Franco had no post. In 1932 he was given command of the infantry brigade of La Coruña. This was only for a short while. "The safety of the Republic" advised his withdrawal. Azaña said to his friends, "I will send him to the Balearic Islands so as to keep him from temptation."

In 1933 he was named military commander over those islands. As he saw the reigning subversion and the ravages caused by the revolution, Franco suffered that depression which has conquered so many patriotic spirits. Was there anything that could be done? He saw that in all branches of public life positive merits and values were being overlooked and swept aside, and others, decrepid, false, and dishonorable, were taking their place and being glorified, recovered, embellished, and exalted by sectarianism. It was the hour of glory for the dangerous and worst elements.

In the military order, Azaña adopted "the freezing-out process." He withdrew and placed at the bottom of the military register the generals, leaders, and officers who had been promoted for merits in war during the period of the Dictatorship, stating that in the procedure legal requirements had not been duly observed.

Franco, in confidence, made known to his intimate friends his restlessness, and told them that he proposed to withdraw from the army to enter politics, to change his local military command by an election, if in that way he could better serve Spain. His friends dissuaded him from the idea. Franco in the army was the supreme and definite guarantee.

What could be defined as a passing spiritual crisis did not last long. Again the general regained the confidence and optimism which rarely abandon him, and faith in the destiny of Spain.

The news concerning Franco's desire to enter politics reached Madrid, and one day, the elections of 1933 already in process, a delegate of the Popular Action presented himself at Palma, in Mallorca, to offer to the general a place on the list of candidates for Madrid, with the promise of reserving for him another place in one of the provinces in order to assure his election. This time Franco did not hesitate. He appreciated the offer but did not accept it. It was by now his firm purpose to stay out of politics.

At that time the general was studying with great interest the landing of James the Conqueror at Mallorca and the conquest of the island by the Aragonese monarch. It was a grand theme for a discussion on strategy, which obsessed him to such an extent that many times he would start the conversation among his friends and companions in order to discuss the event, considering it under present-day conditions. Could it be possible to conquer the Balearics today with modern defenses? The islands continued to be the seduction of the Mediterranean, the brooch of diamonds on the kingly mantle of the azure sea. They were visited by a veritable invasion of tourists who felt a strange curiosity to know the secrets of its shores and to photograph its jutting cliffs.

From historical study Franco went on to examine the reality before his eyes. The Balearics were without defense. The artillery at the Mahon Base was inadequate, for the concussion of the pieces of high caliber rendered useless the light batteries. And the government had entrusted the defense of the Mahon Base to an officer well qualified by his loyalty to Azaña but unqualified as a technician.

Franco worked out a complete plan of defense, devoting himself to this task with the same intelligence and interest which he placed in his work for Spain. With his staff of officers he examined the entire coast line, selecting the sites most appropriate to organize the defense of the island. How many days were spent on foot and on horseback, over mountains and unknown pathless places in the interests of the Mallorcans.

The inhabitants of Pollensa remember well the departure of General Franco and his staff at the break of day, to return at four or five o'clock in the afternoon, sometimes soaked with rain. And one might see in the dining room of the hotel, that table presided over by the general, surrounded by his staff, the table mates in pajamas and riding boots while their rain-soaked uniforms were drying out.

In the following year the plan of defense of the Balearic

Islands was accepted by Minister of War Gil Robles and put into operation. The first thing to be done was the rectification of the faults in the defenses of Mahon.

When, now in the midst of civil war, Franco received news that the Catalonian Communists had landed at Mallorca, he was neither disturbed nor worried. He did not have to dictate long instructions to the general commandant of Mallorca. All he had to do was to direct a radio call to him asking him to carry out the plan of land defense of the island which he had in one of the drawers in his office, drawn up by General Franco himself.

CHAPTER XVI

The October Revolution

FROM the very day that the Socialist Ministry was overthrown, the ousted leaders began to predict the revolution which was to burst out like a volcano in the month of October, 1934. During the summer they orchestrated it with as much boldness as noise. There were inflamed harangues charged with dynamite, angry, and threatening journalistic prose, meetings and gatherings for the purpose of estimating their strength, the marching of well-equipped militia, and a great number of red banners. Pueto, from his seat in congress, had proclaimed the necessity of an armed uprising. Largo Caballero repeated with great fury that the decisive moment was approaching when the Marxists would be ready to play their card, and stated that on this day they could not be accused of being barbarous, for any acts of violence would be justified.

El Socialista described the concentration of soldiers at San Martín de la Vega, and commented: "Uniformed, prepared, in fine military formation, their clinched fists held high and impatient to pull the trigger. The speeches consisted of words that were like gunfire, phrases that were a watchword. . . . In the minds of the listeners, there was a stamp of odium impossible to erase without exemplary and determined violence."

An effort was made to undermine the army with cunning subversive propaganda. All Spain was boiling with strikes which were simply other attempts toward mobilization. The General Workers' Union stated "that it is disposed to procure that the organized working class which it represents, may realize the supreme effort to end the present regime which denies us a hearing, for one which promises to all the broadest union for concrete and definite purposes."

Those who were preparing the revolt knew the efforts that would be necessary to achieve their purpose, and for that reason they did not hesitate to solicit and obtain the assistance of those who by affinity or common interests would be their allies. They were already counting upon the complicity of the sinister personages who survived the failure of their political doctrines, Azaña, Martínez Barrio, Casares Quiroga, Sánchez Román, and Miguel Maura.

In the Basque Provinces, on account of the disappearance of the representative commissions which governed the municipalities, the latter were out of control. Indalecio Prieto, with Socialist deputies and others from the Catalonian group, attracted by the excitement, gathered to stir up the flames of rebellion. There were attempted insurrections in Zumárraga, San Sebastián, and Guernica. "Down with Spain" was the watchword. And one of the principals of Basque separation stated:

"To obtain the liberty of our country we shall stop at nothing. Not even if war is necessary, painful and bloody as it may be. . . . When we constitute the great majority and feel that we have sufficient strength, we shall embark without vacillation upon a war against the Spanish State. I have to defend my nationality at any cost. All is fair in the effort to obtain independence, from throwing a bomb to unchaining the hounds of war — some day there will be much bloodshed."

Along with the uprising of the Basque municipalities there was a revolt of the corporation governments in Catalonia, on the pretext of the interpretation of the *Ley de Cultivos*.

Señor Companys expressed the solidarity of the government over which he presided with the Basque municipalities. "I am not interested," he said, "in knowing whether the movement of the municipalities is legal or not. All that interests me is the triumph of Euzkadi."

On his part, a councilor of the corporation government, Gassols, recommended to the members of a meeting held at Barcelona: "Be ever alert, he who has a scythe with his scythe, he who has tools with his tools, he who can manage a wheel ready to go to the automobile or the airplane."

While the exterior offered this disturbed, agitated, and threatening appearance, underneath moved the currents of conspiracy and illegality. It was spreading, although very little. In San Esteban de Pravia was discovered a supply of smuggled munitions gathered by Socialist deputies. Part of this smuggled goods, seventy-three boxes of ammunition, was confiscated by the internal-revenue officers. In the *Casa del Pueblo* in Madrid the police found an arsenal of pistols and bombs, and in the Stadium in University City the civil guards discovered a great quantity of weapons and ultra-modern war equipment.

Everything had been planned and was in readiness for the order to be given. Only the moment was awaited, and this was not long in arriving. It was the occasion of the ministerial crisis of October 1. Samper resigned and withdrew from congress, because he lacked the support of the minorities who up until that time permitted him to govern as he pleased. On the afternoon of the 4th, Don Alejandro Lerroux formed a new government, in which three members of the *Ceda* figured.[1]

That same night the *Casa del Pueblo* was taking action on the order to Socialist organizations to declare a general revolutionary strike throughout all Spain.

Alcalá Zamora, cognizant of what was taking place, attempted to avert the revolutionary blow with a poor alibi. An agent of the president attempted to placate the Socialist

---

[1] *Ceda*, refers to the Confederation of Rightist Parties, popularly known as the *Ceda* from the initial letters of the Spanish title.

leaders by telling them that the granting of government posts to members of the *Ceda* was only to weaken them and precipitate their downfall. The Socialist politicians refused to accept this explanation and sustained their orders.

On the following day Madrid was the victim of strikes, gagged, and tied up hand and foot. There were no street cars, taxis, or subway. In the bakeries soldiers took the place of bakers. There started a popular reaction against that Red tyranny which subjected and oppressed the city.

As the hours passed the nationalist horizon became more cloudy — the revolutionary strike had taken hold in the provinces. The background of Madrid's dark night was shot through with gunfire. Armed groups were put to flight when discovered on their way to the barracks.

The 6th brought new disturbances. It was now known with certainty that the movement was growing in Asturias and Vizcaya, and possible developments in Barcelona were feared. As the day passed the melancholia in Madrid was converted into anguish. The air seemed to be charged with forebodings. There floated about in the atmosphere something impalpable which was neither light nor sound, but which could be seen and heard; that vague and mysterious presentiment which precedes tragedy, telepathic fluid and breath of an impending catastrophe.

The Barcelona radio, in the hands of the factions, sent over the air waves the news that Companys had proclaimed the "Catalonian State," and from that moment began the frightful and maddening vigil during which the cries of "Catalonians! Dempens! Rise to arms!" were mixed with urgent calls to the Socialists and Communists to crowd the streets, and the music of the Marseillaise, "La Santa Espina," "Els Segadors," a hymn called that of Euzkadi, and a Galician reveille.

It was the signal. At eight o'clock in the evening fighting broke out in Madrid. There were scuffles in front of the commissariats and barracks, and attempts to attack the offices of the Ministry of Government and the Communications Building. The streets were swept with the flash of submachine guns. From the roof tops shots were also fired by those who had joined the conspiracy to create disturbance and alarm, indispensable for the bold blow which was planned against those in power. It was Trotzky's watchword: "Frighten the people with terror before the attack."

The city remained empty, desolate, and aghast. War had been declared and the troops were in the streets. On everyone's lips there was the same question, "What will happen?"

In that moment of uncertainty, panic, and destruction, a man passed through the doorway of the Ministry of War which now was all astir and full of alarm. The man was dressed in civilian clothes. Anyone who could see him at close range saw that the emotion that oppressed and fatigued the city was not reflected in his semblance. A sentinel stopped him and an officer of the guard recognized him. It was General Franco.

At that time Diego Hidalgo was Minister of War. He describes his relations with Franco as follows:

"I met this general in Madrid in the month of February, 1934. I had dealings with him for the first time on my trip to the Balearic Islands, and in those four days I was able to convince myself that his fame was justified.

"Devoted entirely to his profession, he possesses a high degree of all the military qualities, and his activities and capacity for work, his clear judgment, his understanding and his culture are always ready for the call to arms.

"Of his qualities the greatest is his concentration on examining, analyzing, inquiring, and developing problems. A ponderation which impels him to be minute in details, exact in service, correct in observation, strict and demanding in discipline, and at the same time understanding, calm, and devoted.

"He is one of the few men, of those I know, who never

digresses. My conversations with him on military topics, during my stay on those islands, revealed to me, besides, his unusual knowledge. All of the technique of modern warfare is based on the foundation which great generals worked out in the course of history, but its development is based upon the lessons of the Great War, which left not only sorrow and tears, but also great lessons for the future in all branches of life, especially the military.

"Man and the machine unfolded their activities in conformity with new formulas, which did away with a whole series of problems which were believed to have been solved, and which, with the change of premises and integral elements, also changed the technique and its results.

"Science, apart from that called war literature, which fortunately is more deserving of the name literature of peace, has gathered in the works written by the leaders and brains of armies, the teachings and deductions born of new armaments, which necessarily created new methods and procedure."

And Franco, in the silence of his office, has spent many years, years of peace, reading. His study has borne fruit, and today it can be truthfully stated that there is no secret for this soldier in the art of war, elevated to a science by the mind of man.

"He is not merely eloquent, but he is the expounder of problems, and applies theory and generic theses to practice and concrete cases, analyzing coldly the postulates of military science from the point of view of armaments, and studying warmly anything which has to do with the soldier, his morale and his spirit.

"Since he has such a keen mind concerning military maneuvers, it is easily explained why I would like to have near me a critic so singularly capable as an adviser. And I do not know, nor do I care, if I was unfaithful to the protocol by inviting Franco to accompany me to the military maneuvers in the mountains of León.

"At their conclusion, again back in Madrid, in the early days of October, the general, before leaving asked for permission to go to Oviedo on special business. I granted his request gladly, but by chance he was not in Oviedo at the time of the recent developments.

"On learning of these and having to suspend his projected trip, I ordered that he remain to assist me. For apart from his counsel in military matters, due to the fact that he had resided for a long time in Asturias and had family interests there, he knew well not only the wealth and mineral resources but also the coast and all the lines of communication in the region.

"Some persons must have been surprised and must have hidden their displeasure when I decided to retain at my side an adviser who was foreign to the official agencies of the Ministry. But a minister has always the right and the duty to seek freely his adviser, helper, and companion. In trying moments, when the agencies of the Ministry worked under great pressure, it was also perfectly explainable that a minister should surround himself with all those elements which he believed necessary to solve with success and rapidity a grave upsetting of the public order which demanded a very complicated military action, the limits of which were beyond calculation, either in intensity or in extent.

"All those who, with varying degrees of knowledge, commented on my actions in the Ministry of War during the developments in Asturias, have praised the meritorious and efficient work of this general, but no one has had a single word of praise for the minister who appointed him. It is my duty to inform the country that I was that minister, and that if I had not appointed General Franco, with his technical knowledge and admirable qualifications, he would have known the events that were taking place in Asturias through the press in the distant Balearic Islands."

It is curious to note that the very ex-Minister Diego Hidalgo, who thus was proud of having retained General Franco at his side at the time of the October Revolution, remembers with justifiable pride that on the occasion of the first and only vacancy of a division general which occurred during his incumbency in the Ministry of War he promoted Franco, the one whose promotion had been denied by a decree of January 28, 1933, which placed him at the bottom of the list of brigadier-generals.

"According to the letter of the law, on the pages of the *Anuario militar,* General Franco was in one of the last positions, but in my spirit," writes Diego Hidalgo, "he was at the top. . . . And today, no longer in the position that I held, I can well take pride in the thought that it was during my administration that General Franco was promoted to the rank of division general."

When the general entered the office of the minister, the latter said to him, "I have awaited you with great impatience. I have sent several emissaries in search of you. . . . I need you."

"I am at your service," Franco answered.

The minister reached for a bundle of telegrams which he had on his desk and handed it to him. They were the reports of the first devastations produced by the revolutionary hurricane which passed furiously and lashingly through half of Spain. There were strikes, disturbances, and efforts to damage some of the trains. There was a revolutionary movement in Catalonia. The president of the corporate governments had summoned General Batet in order to place his forces at his command. There was an uprising of the miners in Asturias and a march upon Oviedo and Gijón. The munitions factory was fired on.

The minister watched the expression on the face of the reader to see what effect these messages produced. But General Franco remained unperturbed. Only after reading them all, referring to the telegrams concerning Asturias which he held in his hands, he exclaimed, "This is serious. In Oviedo there are insufficient forces to handle the insurrection."

There was a general uprising in the entire mining region. "A movement well planned, which could arm with weapons of war, as had been demonstrated by the recent discoveries of illegally gathered munitions, twenty or thirty thousand men who had already assumed control of a dozen towns in the mining area, and who could obtain control of the two large cities of Asturias, having as their field of action a rough and difficult terrain which the rebels were perfectly acquainted with."

At the same time the garrisons of Oviedo and Gijón could gather together scarcely sixteen hundred men. To send reinforcements from elsewhere would be difficult, for with the reforms made by the different governments under the Republic, the garrisons had been reduced to a minimum.

"A complete unit," Don Diego Hidalgo explained, "could not be removed from any locality without running the risk of leaving it undefended. Add to this the scarcity of communications with Asturias, and the fact that the railroad line and the road from south to north (León to Oviedo), which constitute its best and most rapid means of access, were cut off at the outset, and it can be seen that grave difficulties would be involved in the sending of reinforcements, and in preventing important cities in which the movement might have repercussions from being left to the mercy of providence."

To meet these problems General Franco proposed the sending of troops from Africa.

The minister announced that decision to Mr. Lerroux. The famous proclamation which the leader of the government drew up in the Ministry of State, already vibrated in the atmosphere amid the clash of arms, "Spaniards, at the present moment the rebellion which has come to upset the public order is reaching its apogee."

The government felt confident in its security and was firm. The reason for that feeling of security and optimism was not divulged. But each member of the Ministry made known to his intimates, in order to raise the spirits of those who were downcast and to give them hope, the news that was later learned in political quarters where it had reactive effects.

Franco was in the War Ministry! The whole scene changed. On the turbulent horizon, dense and darkened by the storm, there appeared a ray of light which gave promise of victory. Night no longer brought fear, that terrifying and lugubrious night from which glared the eyes of the wolf packs of anarchy, and which Spain entered with vacillation. A man had taken the helm, and the ship of state faced the tempest with the certainty of emerging victorious.

Franco locked himself up in the Telegraph Office and from there began to organize the battle against the revolution. He was surrounded, as he well knew, by traitors to his cause, in whom he could not place confidence. Masquelet, chief of the Staff of State, was an intimate friend of Azaña. The Ministry was composed of Masons, and for that reason many looked upon Franco as an intruder. Should this general in civilian clothes be permitted to assume power and give orders with supreme authority?

Immediately he began to notice the attempts to nullify his orders and frustrate his plans. The air base at León did not answer to his call. Franco proposed the dismissal of the commander of the base. Batet, in Barcelona, was remiss and digressing. A plan had to be worked out for each garrison.

Franco needed very little advice, for he had at his mind's command all the means of war at Spain's disposal. He mobilized troops and ships. The military commander of Oviedo reported to him that the miners had reached the vicinity of San Lázaro and that the troops were being enclosed in the barracks. He had constant communication with Barcelona, and knew to the moment the steps, actions, and state of mind of General Batet. He conferred with the leaders of the African forces. He chose Lieutenant-Colonel Yagüe, who was on leave in Soria, for the command of the African forces, and the latter went in an autogiro which landed on the beach at Gijón. Each hour that night he won positions, isolated the insurrectionists, and was encircling them.

Those who were working at his side were conquered by the optimism which always radiates from Franco. They saw him tranquil, sure in his decisions, and infallible in his prognostications. All the means to which he had recourse responded with punctuality and exactness. Committed to this laborious task, he was surprised by the light of dawn which beckoned with its silken fingers to the crystal decorations of the room.

It was six o'clock in the morning. A half hour later the following telegram was received from Barcelona:

"Commanding officer Fourth Division to Minister of War: At this moment, six thirty, president of corporative government asked that hostilities cease, surrendering unconditionally to my authority. I take pleasure in communicating to your Excellency knowledge and satisfaction, calling attention to brilliant behavior of all forces under my command, even though at the price of appreciable casualties, which I will report opportunely."

An adjutant awakened the Minister of War to give him this message, because the Minister of War, Don Diego Hidalgo, had only slept since two o'clock in the morning.

In this month of October, 1934, Franco spent day and night in the War Ministry directing the battle against the revolution. It hinged on the vicissitudes of General Bosch's troops which were fighting in the mountains of Campomanes. He lightened the road followed by the column of five hundred men organized in Lugo by General López

Ochoa and also led by him, and he warned him of the danger that awaited him at the narrow passage at Peñaflor, at the outgate of Grado, where were posted the most embattled forces of Asturian anarchy. López Ochoa abandoned this road and went up to Avilés. He conferred daily with Ortiz de Zárate, who was checking the revolutionary uprising in Vizcaya with wise measures. On the 8th, the cruiser *Libertad* was in front of the Santa Catalina hills. Franco, from the Telegraph Office, directed the bombardment.

The commanding officer at Gijón would inform him by telegraph of the artillery setbacks, and Franco would improve and rectify the aim, telling the officers of the ship, by radio, of the mistakes observed and pointing out the objectives.

Franco took the initiative in placing on the commanding terraces of Madrid the best marksmen of the civil guard, aided with reflectors, to combat the hostile rabble on the roof tops.

On the 12th there landed at Gijón the two Banners of infantry and a group of Regulars, who under the command of Lieutenant-Colonel Yagüe began their victorious march to Oviedo, which garrison was to be liberated on the following day.

The outlaws who had been introduced into the Asturian capital by the Soviet regime, fled to the mountains. They had murdered in a cowardly manner, they had robbed the banks, they had set fire to the university, they had tried to sack the cathedral, and they had destroyed entire blocks. Oviedo the martyr, a picture of sorrow and tragedy, was a typical example of Marxist barbarism.

CHAPTER XVII

Franco, Chief of Staff

THE purpose of Gil Robles in obtaining the portfolio of Minister of War was realized in the crisis of May, 1936. Why did Gil Robles insist so much upon fulfilling his desires? Later he explained by saying that this had been his purpose ever since he knew, by the revolution in Asturias, that the policy of Azaña during the last two years had left the army in such bad condition, so defenseless, and in such hands that the nation was in danger of perishing immediately upon a repetition of the revolutionary movement. When the new minister of war took office, the Leftists were disturbed, and frightened their followers with the announcement that a *coup d'état* was brewing. But anyone who knew the true situation in the army knew that it could not dream of such a thing.

Shortly after entering the War Ministry, Gil Robles called a meeting of the division generals, which was attended by Cabanellas (Don Virgilio), Villabrille, Goded, Franco, Gómez Morato, Riquelme, Núñez del Prado, Rodríguez del Barrio, Peña, and others. The meeting lasted five hours, in which the minister submitted a questionnaire to the examination of those gathered and from the information obtained he learned that after four years of the Republic there was scarcely a vestige left of the army. It had been pulverized by the corrosive laws of Azaña. Among other details verified at that meeting were some very conclusive ones such as these: the total munitions in the armories were insufficient to sustain fire for twenty-four hours in a modern war. The troops that went to Campomanes at the time of the revolution in Asturias in 1934 could not carry even first-aid kits. For this reason many soldiers had been victims of gangrene.

The War Ministry proposed to remedy this evil immediately, and so it searched for the most eminent and efficient coworkers. For the position of chief of staff "the general of greatest prestige" was chosen, Franco, who was at that time commanding officer of the army in Morocco. General Fanjul was named assistant secretary, and General Goded director of aeronautics. The Supreme War Council was organized, the presidency of which, during the frequent absences of the minister, was exercised by General Franco.

And there began a work without rest, which was to last six months, only to be checked by the tortuous, crafty, and deceitful politics so pleasing to Don Niceto Alcalá Zamora. The minister had the complete confidence of the General Staff, especially that of his chief and there was not the least divergence in any respect. Their work was harmonious. A sane spirit of justice reigned, in which favoritism had no place.

An enormous amount of work was being done. General Franco appeared at his office at nine o'clock in the morning and remained there until three or three thirty o'clock in the afternoon. An hour later he was again at his desk, continuing work until ten or later in the evening. In the offices of the Ministry they worked as though with the assurance that they were carrying out a work of the greatest national interest and which would redound to the welfare and benefit of Spain.

Out of the chaos to which the army had been reduced by sectarian, unfortunate, unpatriotic politics, it began to revive with gallantry and vigor.

As a fundamental preliminary for the plan outlined, the honorary tribunals, which had been abolished by the constitution, were restored, while the separation from the service for dishonorable acts, and other reservations were regulated, without permitting any of the measures advanced to be attacked on the grounds of injustice or eagerness to persecute, for all those who were ousted were seriously at fault.

Thus Miaja, Mangada, Villalba, Sarabia, Camacho, Riquelme, Viqueiro, Hidalgo de Cisneros, and others were removed from their commands. And in corresponding fashion those soldiers whom the revolution attempted to cast out so that they would be lost and forgotten, were restored to positions of trust and dignity. Colonel Monasterio was restored to the command of a regiment. Varela was promoted to the rank of general. General Mola, who had been disposed of since the establishment of the Republic, was given the job of drawing up a plan of mobilization which was surprising in its perfection and the ability with which it was worked out, and as a consequence he was designated commander-in-chief of the army in Morocco.

The President of the Republic was disturbed by the replacements and the lists of those restored to active service.

"I notice," he said one day to the Minister of War, "that all those favored by promotions or reinstatements are enemies of the Republic."

"All those designated are excellent soldiers," answered Gil Robles.

But the president insisted, "Of the eighty officers named to command troops, only twenty have congratulated me. Here is the list."

"Undoubtedly," answered the minister, "they are unfamiliar with the protocol."

In order to tighten the bonds within the army there was established an interchange among the officers and officials of the different branches of the army. A revision was made of the decorations awarded as a result of the Asturian campaign, and the Military Medal was granted to Lieutenant-Colonel Yagüe.

In a period of economic limitations, a study was made with the purpose of equalizing salaries, and to General Orgaz was entrusted the task of drawing up a plan for military co-operatives which was to correlate with the economic study being carried out by Fanjul and Colmenares.

The influence of hostile propaganda was noticed among the recruits, and from the investigations made it is known that twenty-five per cent of the soldiers were militantly active in revolutionary organizations. Once in the barracks, they formed Communistic groups in order to continue their work. General Franco organized a private information service through which he was able to keep posted on the work of the opposition in the barracks, and through which he was able to make surprising discoveries concerning the work of Russia to undermine Spain.

These investigations contributed in great part to the drawing up of a law of espionage and to the study of a plan to increase the number of volunteers, which would permit greater selection of personnel, with the greatest guarantee of discipline in the regiments.

The subversive propaganda had been spread among the workers in the munitions factories, where lack of discipline was rife. The revolution in Asturias had been a good example and there was no need of further proof. The militarization of the entire personnel working in these factories, and in the aeronautics plants was decreed, with the prohibition of affiliating with revolutionary organizations.

The revolution in Asturias had placed in bold relief the importance of Marxist efforts, and the difficult situation through which Oviedo would pass in a new uprising. To Colonel Aranda, whose exceptional talents as a strategist are well known, was entrusted the command of a mixed brigade, declaring Asturias exempt as a commandancy. On July 21, some maneuvers were held in Riosa in which was studied the rescue of Oviedo, leaving out communication by way of the port of Pajares. The maneuvers were attended by Generals Franco, Goded, and Fanjul.

The work went on uninterrupted, and the intense activity inspired every branch of the Ministry. The Code of Military Justice was revised, the divisions of the government were reorganized, two brigades were created to protect the zone of the Straits and the western boundary. To prepare new officers it was agreed to reopen the General Military Academy and to train engineers specializing in the manufacture of armaments.

The General Staff, under the impulse of the indefatigable and dynamic Franco, was a workshop and laboratory where the structure of the Spanish army was studied and planned out.

In the material order everything was lacking. The ministry was surrounded by desolation and ruin; empty armories, old batteries, and antiquated equipment. The few bombing planes were of 1918 construction, and the bombs of five kilograms weight. The sad condition and penury was the same in artillery, in outfittings, in masks, and helmets.

Very little time was necessary to accomplish a complete transformation. In the month of December a contract was drawn up to acquire the patents on pursuit and bombing planes, which were to be built in Guadalajara. A contest was announced for the construction of twenty-four batteries and the refitting of cannons and anti-aircraft guns.

The soldiers were provided with helmets, the manufacturing of bullets was speeded up, and in Toledo alone three hundred and fifty workers were added to the personnel of the plant, with the purpose of producing eight hundred thousand bullets a day. A study of the manufacturing of gases was inaugurated, and an effort was made to educate the people against chemical warfare.

The Anglo-Italian tension converted the Mediterranean coasts into danger zones, and it was necessary to strengthen the defenses at Cartagena and the Balearic Islands, which in a short time were secure and well fortified.

It was now the middle of December, 1935. There was a plan of rearmament within three years and a complete plan of national defense drawn up by the General Staff. The soldiers without prestige to whom Azaña had confided the duties of greatest responsibility were eliminated. An extraordinary grant of one billion one hundred million had been accepted by the Council of Ministries, which was to be spent almost entirely in Spain.

The plan had all the elements essential for a grandiose work. But in a Spain shot through with revolution it was impossible. So impossible that it did not even get started. On December 19 the crisis was declared. It was the last crisis. After it came the storm of blood and bullets.

The Minister of War was the recipient of an unforgettable farewell on the part of the personnel of the Ministry. General Franco bid him farewell in the name of all the rest:

"Never has the army felt itself to be in better hands than under this administration. Honor and discipline, the basic concepts, have been restored."

And he added, "To signify to what extent honesty had been the only rule of action of the War Ministry, it is sufficient to relate a simple episode: There was a proposal for an appointment. Three names were under consideration, three officers whose names had been brought together by the same circumstances and who had the same qualifications. The Minister of War had to decide from among these three names. I pointed out that any one of them was capable and could undertake the duty brilliantly, but in all honesty I told him that one of the officers was recommended by nearly all the friends of the minister himself, by the chamber of deputies, and by men high in the army. The minister answered, 'Discarding those factors, whom would you designate?' I answered him, 'The three are of equal merits. I would select the oldest.' The minister did not hesitate for a moment and ordered, 'Very well, the oldest.' Such had been our War Ministry."

That army destroyed by the politics of the previous two years, that is, by favoritism, intrigue, and injustice, and handled by the unfortunate military cabinet created by Azaña, began to be restored in six months of honest administration, in which the martial virtues began to shine again, merit was recognized, and those things prejudicial or dangerous to the nation were discarded. The work of reorganization advanced rapidly, and it was evident that it would not be long before the army would again be the national institution, strong and respected, against which those who had taken upon themselves to ruin Spain could not prevail.

But the plan to rearm the army could not be tolerated by the revolution. "The revolutionary elements," said Gil Robles, "could no longer tolerate, nor permit the continuation of this work, because they saw that this reorganization of the army was beginning to be carried out, and it presented to the revolution an insurmountable barrier."

Alcalá Zamora, docile pawn, gave in again, and surrendered the fort. Into it entered, on a Masonic horse, new Trojan artifice, the languid, weak, and malign figure of Portela, that human specter, that element of a ghost story whom fate had chosen for the most tragic of deeds; namely, to open the gates of Spain to the four horsemen of the apocalypse.

CHAPTER XVIII

1936: The Reign of Terror

THE revolution was not crushed in October. A weak and acquiescent government, together with a protection which seemed more like complicity on the part of the President of the Republic, allowed the leaders of that insurrection against Spain to go free. The roots remained intact, and it was not long before they again became active.

The elections of February, 1936, provided the opportunity for this resurrection. All the revolutionary parties in Spain, from the less enthusiastic that called themselves left-wing Republicans to those of the infra-Red zone, joined forces beforehand. They entered into this conglomeration, however, with the secret and mutual hope of deceiving each other. The left-wing Republicans expected to reap the fruits of victory, once it had been achieved, unhampered by their ultra-radical allies, these to be sloughed off in the course of time. However, the Socialists, as Alvarez del Vayo pointed out in an address at Málaga, entered into this alliance in the hope that their bourgeois allies, the left-wing Republicans, would pave the way for the more rapid achievement of their aims "after breaking down the resistance of capitalism and demilitarizing the army."

In this alliance, which came to constitute the Popular Front, and which was to be the cause of so much misfortune in Spain, there was particular care exercised to fix as the indispensable basis for negotiations the resolution that amnesty be granted to all those jailed for their participation in the revolution of October (1934), that those who had lost their positions as a result of this insurrection be reinstated, and that punishment be meted out to those who in the capacity of public officials were responsible for the suppression of the revolt.

The elections were held on February 16, 1936. And in spite of the fact that the counterrevolutionary parties — in the face of extensive and discouraging abstentions in their ranks — commanded a popular majority of over 400,000 votes, the adherents of the Popular Front, from seven o'clock in the evening of that very day, launched a series of frenzied demonstrations, proclaiming their triumph. And from that very moment the fraud began. The majority was gradually disintegrated, gradually subtracted from, to end, but a few weeks later, with the scandalous robbery of over eighty seats in parliament, accomplished by action of the Parliamentary Commission, which in some cases, notably of the deputies from Cuenca and Granada, added insult to injury.[1]

Thus did the revolutionaries assume power, and there was

---

[1] ". . . in spite of the aid of the Syndicalists, the Popular Front did not obtain legally more than slightly over 200 seats in a parliament of 473 deputies. It became the most important minority, but it did not have an absolute majority. It succeeded in obtaining it, however, by two quick moves.

"First, from the 17th of February, as a matter of fact from the evening of the 16th, the Popular Front, without waiting for the completion of the counting of the votes, and the announcement of the results, which was to take place before the provincial committees of verification on the 20th, unleashed a campaign of disorder in the streets and clamored for power through violence. There was a crisis; many governors resigned. At the instigation of irresponsible ringleaders, the mobs took possession of the electorial certificates, and in many places the results were falsified.

"Second, having thus obtained a majority, it was easy to make it a crushing one. Strengthened by a bizarre alliance with the reactionary Basques, the Popular Front appointed a committee in charge of the validation of parliamentary credentials, which acted in a purely arbitrary manner. All the election certificates of certain provinces in which the Right was victorious were annulled, and defeated candidates of the Left were declared elected. Many other deputies of the Right were expelled from Parliament. This whole procedure was not merely the blind passion of sectarian politics: it was the execution of a deliberate and widespread plan. . . .

Niceto Alcalá Zamora,
Former President of the Spanish Republic."

In *Journal de Genève*, Geneva, January 17, 1937.

no longer any obstacle to block their despotic designs. Their first step was to remove Niceto Alcalá Zamora from the presidency of the Republic, with less decorum than that usually accorded a servant, in order to raise in his stead Manuel Azaña, who resigned himself to this coup with the deepest of sorrow, abandoning the premiership to lock his lordly melancholy in the National Palace and the royal summer homes of the northern coast.

The road was wide and free. And so the vanguards of the Popular Front overran Spain. From the electoral purge, those who had taken part in the revolution of October emerged haughty and triumphant, as well as those who were serving criminal terms; those who had shocked the world with their excesses, instigators of crime, assassins, robbers, all those elements of ferocity and hatred which burst forth in times of revolution and disorder — these sprang forth in great hordes, just as the mud of a great pond can blacken all the surface when its tranquil waters are stirred.

Those who were under the protection accorded members of parliament exhibited boundless audacity. From the moment that they received their official passes granting them free traveling privileges, they devoted themselves to agitation in the cities and villages throughout the length and breadth of the country, intoxicating the masses with the wine of Russia, and embittering them against all existing institutions. And in their wake they left a trail of hatred; seeds of revolution and furrows of despair, soon to be drains of fire and bloodshed as well.

Spain was to be at peace no more. From the capital of the Republic to the tiniest rural village, every town trembled with the spirit of extermination and was rocked by a mad storm of passion. It was a headlong race to reach the depths of fury.

"When the hour of revenge is at hand, we shall not leave one stone upon another of this Spain that we shall

destroy, to rebuild our own," promised Largo Caballero
in Zaragoza.

"We want a revolution," screamed frenzied Margarite
Nelken, "but not even the Russian one can serve as our
model for we need gigantic pyres that will glow around the
earth, and torrents of blood that will dye the seas red."

"The Rightists," added *El Socialista,* "are alarming their
adherents with the memory of October, telling them that it
was a revolution. They are deceiving themselves. That was
only a trial for what is coming, for what Spain is yet to
know."

Bold prophecies and hair-raising threats emanated daily
from the Communist and Syndicalist press, printed solely
for the purpose of inflaming the passions of their
readers.

Together with this propaganda, originating in and directed from Moscow, where in August, 1935, at the International Communist Congress, the formation of the Popular
Front had been agreed upon, there came forth another
which emanated from the streets, openly and ostentatiously.
It consisted of the demonstrations and parades of the mili-
tiamen in uniform, who raised clenched fists in defiance
and unfurled red banners bearing the symbols of Communism. Mobilizations were carried out under various pre-
texts; at times to demand the release of any *gerfalcon* of
Communism imprisoned abroad, be he Thaelmann or
Prestes; at times to promote the celebration of a "Red Olympiad" in Barcelona in opposition to what they called the
"Brown Olympiad" of Berlin; and interspersed among these
political and athletic demonstrations there were organized
general strikes in order to test the functioning of the local
committees and the district radio stations. At times they
went even further, as on that day of revolt which they inspired by spreading the false rumor that Rightists were dis-
tributing poisoned candy among the children, and which
ended in assaults on churches and convents; and that night

of terror that saw the churches of San Luis and San Ignacio and the newspaper plant of *La Nación* go up in flames, great flaming torches in the resplendent light of which the capital of Spain could read the tragedy of its future.

There were assaults, attacks, and useless strikes. There was arson, forcible seizure of city factories, sacking and seizure of rural farms. There were holdups on the highways, political murders and much fighting; and every day, that indispensable and endless list of civil guards and army officers dismissed, shifted or put on waiting orders, and accused of being reactionaries, Fascists, or of lukewarm disposition toward the regime.

There was more tragedy and disorder in one day under the Popular Front government than under three months of normal rule.

As an example, *El Diario Vasco* of San Sebastián, in the issue of May 14, contained the following news items despite an iron-clad censorship:

"*Vigo.* Fascist youths were shot at. An army officer, intervening in their behalf, drew forth more fire. The officer finally had to hide in his home, which was then burned. The civil guard, who attempted to restore order, were fired upon. Many were killed and wounded."

"*Jaca.* A Communist councilman was attacked by an army officer. Mobs gathered and attempted to lynch the soldier. Serious disturbances ensued."

"*Coruña.* The parish priest of Roderio was beaten. He was then bound and exhibited to the populace. The parish house of Horro was assaulted."

"*Santander.* The churches of Campuzano, Ganzo, Cortiguera, and Zurita were burned."

"*Barcelona.* The police have arrested more than forty persons accused of being Fascists."

"*Valencia.* Serious disorders broke out in Alcira. The churches of San Juan and Santa Catalina have been burned, as well as a convent, a children's school, and the house of the notary. The disorders are spreading to the neighboring villages."

"*Oviedo*. The miners' strike is spreading. By next week 30,000 men will be on strike."

"*Valencia*. A general strike has been called in Sueca."

"*Fuentelapiedra*. Disorders. The parish church has been burned. The incendiarists were led by the mayor and the chief of police."

"*Córdoba*. A general strike is in progress in Zueros. The Civil Guard was stoned in the streets."

"*Oviedo*. In this city and Gijón, arrests of Rightists accused of conspiracy against the regime continue."

"*Teruel*. In Alfambra several youths accused of being Fascists were shot at and jailed."

"*Priego*. Street fighting. Three were wounded, and many were arrested."

"Holdups in Oviedo and Granada."

This was one day under the Popular Front, as filtered by the government censorship.

In April, Calvo Sotelo submitted for publication in the *Diario de Sesiones* of the cortes a list of outrages, attacks, and burnings of churches, attacks on individuals, and attacks on and burnings of newspapers, political centers, clubs, and private dwellings, a list which filled many pages. It was the résumé of what had happened in Spain from February 17 to March 31.

Attack and destruction: political centers, 58; public and private institutions, 72; private dwellings, 33; churches, 36. Total, 199.

General strikes, 11; riots, 169; shootings, 39; attacks, 85; killed, 74; wounded, 345.

In his speech of May 6 in the cortes, Calvo Sotelo supplemented this list with acts of violence, fighting, bloodshed, arson, and destruction from the 1st of April to May 4. The thirty-four days of the Popular Front may be synthesized in the following figures:

Killed, 42; wounded (200 seriously), 216; strikes, 38; bombings, 53; partial or complete destruction by fire, principally of churches, 52; holdups, attacks, and attempts at murder, 99.

Calvo Sotelo added that there was almost an infinite variety of acts contained in these figures; a chromatism of truly sinister implication, in which could be detected every sign of malice, of unchecked barbarity, of savagery, and of complete absence of public authority, if not complicity. No type of crime imaginable by the most frenzied mind was absent from this terrible list. In connection with the occurrences and others preceding them, the police had arrested great numbers of persons, estimated variously at from 8,000 to 10,000, many of them for being, for seeming to be, or for having been Fascists.

The denunciation of these disorders and outrages day after day in the cortes by the Rightist minorities, and the protests against these barbarians who were vandalizing Spain, were useless. Casares Quiroga himself had declared the government belligerent against Fascism; yet, far from discouraging anarchy, he encouraged it by his conduct and favored it with all the forces at his command.

In his final speech of July 16, Gil Robles read the statistics, positively authenticated, on acts of violence and destruction which had been committed from June 16 to July 13. They read as follows:

Church-burnings, 10; other burnings, 19; parish priests outraged, 9; robberies and confiscations, 11; demolishment of public crosses, 5; dead, 61; wounded, 224; holdups, 17; assaults and seizure of farms, 32; confiscations of other property, 16; assaults and burnings of political centers, 10; bombings, 74; petardings, 58; bottles containing inflammable liquids hurled at private dwellings, 7; general strikes, 15; partial strikes, 129.

This was the fearful chaos in which Spain was living.

"We are in a state of anarchy," declared the ex-Minister Ventosa of the Catalan Lliga, "without precedent in the history of any nation." It was a war in which one side had control of all the means and arms of warfare, while to the other side was left the only sad recourse of awaiting its annihilation.

For this state of anarchy the government was entirely to blame. It encouraged it, to the full satisfaction of the revolutionaries, who found fertile ground in it for the development of their plans.

"Everything is progressing to our satisfaction," proclaimed *Claridad,* the Marxist daily. "We are approaching the ultimate implications of our electoral triumph. Shall we return to legality, as the Rightists demand? To what legality? We know no law but that of revolution."

And from the stage of the *Teatro Europa,* Largo Caballero proclaimed that Spain was living under the sign of "Red October." "The victory of the 16th of February was motivated by the revolution of October, and everything we are doing today is inspired by the revolution of October. Let no one come to tell us that an absolutely legal victory was won because that is not true. If there had not been a 4th of October, there never would have been a 16th of February, nor would the left-wing Republicans be now in power. Be aware, one and all, that our inspiration is October, and that we shall tolerate no treason to this cause. Because the new regime, which is rapidly drawing near with giant strides, shall not be held back, neither by bayonets nor cannon."

In anticipation of this regime, the so-called Revolutionary Alliances were organized, a type of Popular Front "unhampered by the bourgeois residue." Proletarian parties exclusively were permitted to enter them, while the left-wing Republicans, excluded from the new organizations, observed from a position of public trust and power the development of this revolutionary organization, consenting to it. It was their obligation, for they were not to forget that power was given them precisely through the promise that they would grant freedom of action to their allies, for their own ulterior motives.

The radical conventions which were held in the various provinces resolved on the union of all Marxists. The Assembly of the Confederación General de Trabajo (C.G.T.), held in Zaragoza on May 14, "approves the revolutionary alliance, which shall have as its immediate aim the destruction of the present regime to the end that first libertarian Communism, and then Anarchism be established as the definitive form of government."

The convention of the Union General Trabajadora (U.G.T.), held in San Sebastián on June 27, declared itself a part of the Marxist unification, and declared that the proletariat would attain its integral emancipation by armed insurrection, destroying the bourgeois Republic and establishing the dictatorship of the proletariat.

It was the same everywhere. August 1, "Red Day," was already set aside to be celebrated by a general mobilization of revolutionary organizations throughout all Spain, not excepting even the smallest villages, and this trial was to be the definitive one. The order to repeat it with sickles and weapons would not be slow in coming. The carefully laid plans from Communist headquarters for the assassination of the generals and officers of the army were well known. The military were to disappear, when the moment came, in a mass slaughter, for which there had been charted a careful distribution of assassins.

The propaganda in the press and in public meetings was daily becoming more furious. The militia were being drilled in the fields adjoining every city, under the direction of army officers. The presence in Spain of specialists in organizing terrorism and assassination was charged. The French press denounced the importation of these men into Spain specifically. "Among others there arrived," declared *Le Matin,* "a special confidant of Stalin, comrade Ventura, who declared before the last meeting of the Comintern, 'The day is soon coming when we shall avenge the dead of Asturias. We will apply the severest forms of terror, and exterminate the bourgeoisie.' "

Spain, livid and panting, exhausted her energy trying to free herself from these serpents that tortured her as they did Laocoön of old, twining themselves to strangle her within their coils. This time the revolution felt sure of its triumph.

The news burst forth like a flash of lightning in the night. Consternation gripped Spain. José Calvo Sotelo had been assassinated. But to say this is to tell only half of the truth. The leader of the Monarchist minority was forcibly taken from his home at dawn by men wearing uniforms of the police force, of which they were members. He was then placed in an automobile of the assault guards, and in it he was killed. To add insult to injury, his body was left at the gates of the cemetery.

The crime was such a monstrous one that it seemed bred of a world of nightmare and deranged minds, impossible to explain, for no language has yet been devised which could describe it. In any organized or the least bit civilized society, such an abominable crime as this is not committed. But if perchance it does occur, the eyes and hearts of men turn up to those in authority, that they may bring the transgressors to justice. This consolation was denied to Spain of 1936. She could not demand justice from those in authority. How could she, when the government itself had planned the crime, which was merely one more in a long list committed in the face of its indifference or with its connivance? The Monarchist minority, "Renovación Española," withdrew from parliament, "because it will not associate with a government of assassins."

Calvo Sotelo had been singled out by the revolution as one

of its principal victims. A certain deputy answering to the name of Galarza, who seemed to seek celebrity at the price of any excess or inhumanity, defended the assassination of Calvo Sotelo in the cortes. Eight days before the crime the leader of the Monarchist minority had confided to Gil Robles that he feared for his life, complaining of a suspicious shifting in his bodyguard, from which the regular police had been removed and had been substituted by assault guards. But the premier of the Spanish government himself had threatened Calvo Sotelo. The leader of the Monarchists had replied in the following manner:

"My shoulders are broad, Casares Quiroga. Your Honor is a very eloquent speaker, always ready with challenging gestures and words of threat. I have heard you make three or four speeches in my whole life, all three or four of them from that blue bench [where the cabinet sits during the sessions of the cortes], and in all of them there has always been a threatening note. Very well, Casares Quiroga, I consider myself notified of Your Honor's threats. Your Honor has made of me a subject, and therefore not only active but passive in the responsibilities which may arise from my own acts. Casares Quiroga, I repeat, my shoulders are broad. I gladly accept all the responsibilities that may arise from my own acts, and any other responsibilities, if they are for the good of my country and for the glory of Spain. More you cannot ask of me. I say what St. Dominic of Silos answered to a Castilian king, 'My lord, you can take my life, but you can do no more.' And I prefer to die gloriously than to live in dishonor."

His party, the "Renovación Española," after accusing the government withdrew from parliament. On the 16th of July Gil Robles delivered a speech in which he laid on the government of Casares Quiroga the moral responsibility of patronizing a policy of violence that gave support to the assassins.

"Every day," he declared, "on the part of the majority in parliament, on the part of newspapers inspired by you, there are scares and threats, threats to destroy your adversaries in order to carry out a policy of extermination. You are practicing it daily. Men are being killed, wounded, insulted, intimidated, fined, and attacked. . . . This period of our history will be recorded as the most shameful period of any regime, any system of government, any nation."

And later he added these words, in which the leader of the *Ceda* expressed his disillusionment and lack of confidence in the idea that Spanish politics could be developed through legal channels and be directed by civilized norms:

"We came into these cortes, though there were many voices which told us there was no place for us here, in order to assure the normal function of the existing agencies and institutions; but little by little we are being forced from that legality; little by little we see that all our efforts are falling upon dead soil; little by little, the Spanish masses are realizing that they will achieve nothing through democratic means. Let no one tell us that we are conspiring against the regime or are creating a state of mind favorable to such conspiracy. In the ranks of the Leftists, if not in the speeches in parliament, certainly in its corridors, in conversation, in their newspapers, there is constant talk of intents or attempts at dictatorship. The radical Labor parties are proclaiming that the height of their ambition is to establish the dictatorship of the proletariat. When you, who call yourselves the representatives of genuine democracy, are talking of dictatorship why do you think it strange if these oppressed people are beginning to think of violence; not in order to crush their opponents, but in order to free themselves from the tyranny with which you are oppressing them? You will be the only ones responsible if such a movement bursts forth in Spain. We brought with us to the elections of the 16th of February the spirit of great national political parties imbued with the fullness of the democratic spirit. If that spirit is dying out in Spain, it is not through any fault of ours, but the sole responsibility of the government; for that which once could have been possible degenerated, in your hands, into but another farce."

What steps did the government take against the assassins? It limited itself to the declaration that the instigators of the crime were being sought, while it was common knowledge in Madrid that the criminals were at liberty, and were being congratulated for their deed. More true, on the other hand, was the fact that every newspaper editor had received secret orders from the government censor prohibiting mention of even the fact that Calvo Sotelo had been assassinated. Neither were there permitted any commentaries on the crime, nor the least reference, in news reports, to the participation in the deed of one officer of the civil guard and officers and men of the assault guards. But this iron censorship was not enough. There remained another item to be suppressed. The publication of the funeral announcement was prohibited.

To these journalistic precautionary measures there were added other political ones. All the Rightist political centers in Spain were closed. Men were arrested by the hundreds. Police stations were jammed to overflowing with reputable people taken by surprise in their homes, who were clapped into cells without a word of explanation. Thousands of persons in Madrid lived like fugitives, hiding, sleeping in a different house every night, fearful of falling into the hands of the man-hunting officers of the law.

Those were hot, intolerable, July nights, made endless by insomnia, accompanied by the sound of automobiles that went, like meteors, in search of innocence, or came with human prey to darkened cells. Nights of fever, ennervating, pulsing with a hurried, anguished beat, patroled by Socialist and Communist militia, pistol-girded, bragging, challenging, bloodthirsty, drugged with that hatred lauded by their press as a sign of Marxist loyalty. Suffocating nights, unnerving, boiling, endless, in that sad Madrid of July, 1936, troubled by mysterious premonitions and gnawed by uneasiness. Suddenly that city turned vicious as a snakes' nest, and men's eyes stared suspiciously, and the air was heavy with electric tension, and the flight of augury blackened all the skies. The flame was flickering on the fuse and was drawing nearer to the powder charge.

CHAPTER XIX

Franco Faces the Revolution

ON THAT Sunday afternoon of February 16, 1936, the mobs, faithful to the watchword of the revolution, poured out into the streets. Completely ignoring the true results of the elections, they proclaimed themselves the victors. They had been thus instructed. Three hours after the end of the balloting, they were to give themselves up to jubilant and frenzied demonstrations, demanding complete power, the liberation of the prisoners of October, 1934, and the heads of certain politicians. The night augured serious street fighting.

General Franco called General Pozas, director of the civil guard, to his side and said to him, "I presume that you are aware of what is happening."

"I do not believe anything is happening," answered Pozas indifferently.

"That is precisely why I have called you, to inform you that the mobs are in control of the streets, and that in furtherance of their revolutionary aims, they are trying to extract from these elections consequences which are neither implicit nor even implied in the results, and I fear that disorders will break out here as well as in the provinces, if they have not broken out already."

"I believe your fears are exaggerated."

"I hope that is the case; but lest they are not, I should like to remind you that we live under established laws. These I accept, and they oblige us, though I for one am opposed to this system, to accept the results of the ballot box. But if these results are changed in the slightest degree, they are unacceptable by reason of the same electoral and democratic theory."

"They will not be changed, I assure you."

"I believe that you are promising something which you will not be able to carry out. It would be more efficacious if persons of responsibility and those of us who hold definite posts in the service of the state and the established regime keep in close touch with one another to make sure that the mobs will not take us by surprise."

The director of the civil guard did not care to listen to these words. "I repeat, all this is not as important as you seem to think. In my opinion, what is occurring is merely a legitimate expression of Republican joy. I see no reason for expecting anything serious."

In the face of Pozas' servile and adulatory attitude toward the revolutionaries, General Franco realized that he could not count on him in any emergency.

As the evening slowly went on, crowded with threats, omens, and hoarse shouting, General Franco was notified by several well-informed friends that Red pressure had already begun to make itself felt in the form of disturbances in many localities, that more serious disorders were feared, and that Portela, in a depressed state of mind, was only a puppet in the hands of the revolution.

It was nearly three o'clock in the morning when Franco called upon the Minister of War, General Molero, who was sleeping. He awakened him. Molero began to talk before he had completely recovered from the drowsiness of his first sleep. He was astonished at the things General Franco told him.

"And what do you think I can do?"

"The first thing to do is to take a proclamation of a state of war to the cabinet."

"Does Portela know it?"

"I shall speak to him right now."

He did speak to him, and at the meeting of the cabinet

on Monday it was decided to proclaim a state of war throughout all Spain. General Franco had drawn up the necessary orders, which he put into effect as soon as he was informed by telephone of the action of the ministers. At the same time he began a series of conferences with the commanding generals, which he was obliged to interrupt in view of an urgent message delivered to him by an assistant that Portela wished to see him immediately. Portela had called him in order to communicate to him the annoyance of the President of the Republic upon learning that the Ministry had decided to proclaim a state of war. The president had also announced that he would not tolerate it, for he considered it a provocation to the people.

"And what do you think?" asked Franco.

"I obey the orders of Alcalá Zamora," answered Portela.

Portela was resigning himself to this and to much more. However, at the special request of General Franco, he held a meeting with him on that same night through the efforts of Natalio Rivas. The general strongly encouraged Portela to declare a state of war despite the opposition of Niceto Alcalá Zamora, and advised him to take any steps which might be necessary to suppress the anarchy which was taking possession of Spain.

Portela was opposed to the suggestion. "I am an old man. I am an old man," he repeated. "The course which you are proposing that I follow is beyond my strength. I can tell you that you are the only one who is making me waver. But I cannot. That remains for a man stronger than I."

"You are the ones who have plunged the nation into this crisis, and it remains your duty to save it."

"And why not the army?" asked Portela suddenly.

"The army," replied Franco, "has not even the moral unity necessary to follow out such a course. Your intervention is necessary, because you have authority over Pozas, and you are still in control of the unlimited resources of the State, with all the public authorities at your command, as well as the aid which I promise you, and which you can count on definitely."

Portela was nervous and uneasy. He rose from his chair, took a few steps, and sat down again. He seemed unnerved, feverish. He was anxious to end this struggle. He concluded by saying, "Let me consult my pillow."

General Franco replied, "I know already what it will say to you; that you should not. Whereas the situation is so urgent that there is no time for consultations or delays."

Portela repeated, "Let me think it over."

The next day, this reflection delivered the expected results. The head of the government made it known to General Franco that the situation was not as grave as he had painted it, that everything was to be adjusted by a ministry of Leftists, and that there was no reason to fear the catastrophic future which the general predicted.

Meanwhile Portela was plotting with Martínez Barrio, the "Grand Orient" of Masonry. The latter was keeping a close watch on the head of the government, and did not let him out of his sight for an instant. The two were conversing when General Pozas burst into the room.

"Mr. President," exclaimed the new arrival, his words distorted by emotion, "I have important news for you. I know with absolute certainty that General Franco and General Goded are inciting the garrisons to revolt."

Martínez Barrio simulated great astonishment and indignation at that farcical scene, which he himself had arranged.

"This is intolerable. We cannot wait a moment longer."

Pozas threatened, "The civil guard will oppose any uprising on the part of the military."

The director of the civil guard was presuming that a few short months with him in charge of that renowned body had sufficed to dishonor and disintegrate it.

That interview was the kiss of Judas. On that day was arranged the surrender of Spain to the revolutionaries.

The Popular Front thus assumed power. The decree

sending General Goded and General Franco away from Madrid was not delayed. One was sent as the Commander-General of the Balearics, and the other to the Canary Islands. Azaña repeated anew that by sending them away to distant posts he was removing them from temptation.

Before departing to his destiny, General Franco called on Alcalá Zamora and Azaña. His interview with the former was of long duration. Franco pointed out the dangers threatening Spain, and the lack of equipment with which to oppose the victorious revolution. Alcalá Zamora smiled between blindness and simplicity.

"The revolution," he said, "was crushed in Asturias."

"Remember, Mr. President," answered Franco, "what it cost to suppress it in Asturias. If the assault is repeated throughout the entire nation, it will be very difficult to suppress it, because the army does not have the necessary equipment, and because generals determined that it shall not be suppressed have been reinstated in command. Gold braid means nothing when he who displays it has no authority, prestige, or competence, the indispensable foundations of discipline."

Alcalá Zamora minimized all this, refusing to comprehend that language of loyalty and honor. He gesticulated incredulously. He shook his head from side to side. The general arose. The President of the Republic gave him leave.

"Don't worry, General. Don't worry. In Spain there will be no Communism."

"One thing that I am sure of," answered Franco, "and which I can answer truthfully, is that whatever the contingencies that may arise here, wherever I am there will be no Communism."

His interview with Azaña was shorter and more brusque. In those days the Premier spent his time pacifying the people with the promise of a moderate and semibourgeois revolution. Franco's predictions were received with a self-satisfied and sardonic smile.

"You are making a mistake in sending me away," the general pointed out regretfully, "because I could be of more service to the army and to the peace of the country by remaining in Madrid."

Azaña answered, "I have no fear of insurrections. I knew all about Sanjurjo's, and I could have prevented it, but I preferred to see it end in disaster."

He himself was the revolution, and he cared little for the advice of generals.

Franco, neither with the idea of conspiracy nor because of hostility toward the regime, but having in mind Spain alone, and the dangers confronting her, decided to hold several interviews which he considered necessary. He held one with General Mola and General Varela, to whom he entrusted the task of maintaining permanent connections with the generals of those divisions which deserved full confidence and with those military elements of the highest responsibility whom, by reason of their positions of command, it would be expedient to keep enlightened on the march of events, so as to be prepared for any emergency which might arise. He named a person in whom he had full confidence to maintain through him the contacts which he considered indispensable, from his post in the Canary Islands.

During those same days, and only a short time before José Antonio Primo de Rivera was imprisoned, he talked with him in the house of an intimate and devoted friend of the general. Primo de Rivera explained to him the position of the "Falange Española," giving him information concerning the strength which it had at its command in Madrid and in the provinces for a given moment. The general advised him to keep in touch with Lieutenant-Colonel Yagüe, whom Primo de Rivera knew by virtue of having had an interview with him on a previous occasion in that same house. General Franco held other discussions with personages of pronounced influence in certain political circles.

From the Canary Islands General Franco witnessed the drama unfolding itself in Spain. Every day the chaos was more profound, and the havoc greater. When the elections were repeated in Cuenca, the conservative parties again offered him a place on their lists, but Franco declined it publicly. Political passions were fanned to a white heat, and he believed that nothing noble or effective could be expected from the existing parliament. Nor did he believe in the sincerity of the voting.

"When the funds of the workers' organizations," he said, "are devoted to political bribery, the purchase of arms and munitions, and the hiring of gunmen and assassins, democracy, as represented by universal suffrage, has ceased to exist."

What worried him particularly was the reduction of the number of officers of the army and the civil guard which the Minister of War was carrying out; a decimation which was reducing the possibility of resistance because the majority of those being expelled or demoted were the men most favorably inclined to that movement which every day was becoming more inescapable and imminent.

It was then that General Franco decided to write a letter to the Minister of War with the secret intention of restraining that headlong course of destitution and displacement, which definitely endangered the success of the movement in certain provincial capitals and regions. Franco succeeded to a large extent in doing this, for upon receiving the letter, the destructive wrath of the minister subsided. The letter, which bears the date June 23, read as follows:

"Honorable Minister:

"So serious is the state of uneasiness which the recent military decrees seem to have produced among the officers of the army, that I would incur a grave responsibility and disloyalty were I not to inform you of my impressions of the state of the army at the present moment and of the dangers to its discipline brought about by the absence of inner satisfaction and the moral and material uneasiness which can be discerned, without obvious demonstration, in the ranks of the officers and petty officers. The recent decrees reinstating in the army the generals and officers sentenced in Catalonia [for their participation in the revolution of October, 1934], and the more recent decree transferring, through ministerial caprice, positions formerly allotted by the rule of seniority, which had not been broken since the reorganization of the army in June, 1917, have awakened a spirit of uneasiness among the great majority of the army. The news of the incidents which took place in Alcalá de Henares, and the disturbances and provocations on the part of extremist elements which preceded them, together with the reassortment of the garrisons, have undoubtedly produced a feeling of dissatisfaction; this feeling, unfortunately and crudely manifested in moments of confused thinking, has been interpreted as a collective transgression producing serious consequences among the generals and officers who participated in those acts, and occasioning sorrow and regret among the ranks of the military.

"All this, most excellent sir, apparently makes manifest either the insufficient information which must possibly be reaching you in this respect, or the ignorance which those elements of the military who are collaborating with you may have with respect to the intimate moral problems of the army. I should not want this letter to detract from the good names of those who inform you and advise you in the military field, for they may sin through ignorance; but I do feel that I can say, with the responsibility of my position and the seriousness of my vocation, that the decrees so far published show obviously that the information which prompted their promulgation is contrary to reality and at times contrary to the interests of the nation, presenting the army to you in a vicious light far removed from reality.

"Those who have been recently removed from their commands and thus thwarted in their careers, are for the most part generals of brilliant record and highly respected in the army. These, as well as others of great trustworthiness and distinction, have been replaced by men who are considered by fully 90 per cent of their comrades-in-arms to be of inferior qualifications. Those who approach our present institutions to flatter them and to demand the reward for their collaboration with them are not necessarily more loyal to them, for those same ones distinguished themselves in former years under the Dictatorship and under the Monarchy. Those who paint the army as hostile to the Republic are not telling the truth; those who are accusing the army of conspiracies in their turbid passions are deceiving you; those who are misrepresenting the uneasiness, the dignity, and the patriotism of the army, making it appear as the symbol of conspiracy and dissatisfaction, are rendering a miserable service to their country.

"Out of the absence of impartiality and justice in the public service in the administration of the army in 1917, there arose the Juntas of Military Defense. It could be virtually said that today, in spirit at least, the Military Juntas are a reality. The writings which are clandestinely appearing with the initials U.M.E. and U.M.R. are convincing symptoms of their existence and heralds of future civil strife if steps are not taken to prevent it. I consider it easy to prevent it with measures of consideration, impartiality, and justice. That movement of collective insubordination of 1917, motivated, in large part, by favoritism and arbitrary caprice in the matter of promotions, was produced under circumstances similar to, though perhaps worse than, those which exist today in the ranks of the army. I will not hide from your Excellency the dangers inherent in this state of collective conscience at the present moment, in which is joined to professional uneasiness the uneasiness felt by all good Spaniards confronted by the grave problems facing their country.

"Though many miles removed from the Peninsula, reports

do not fail to reach me, through various channels, which affirm that the state of mind which can be noticed here exists equally, if not to a greater extent, not only in the peninsular garrisons, but also among all the military forces charged with maintaining public order. As one who knows the meaning of discipline, to the study of which I have devoted many years, I can assure you that such is the spirit of justice that reigns in the ranks of the military, that any harsh measure which is unjustified produces self-defeating consequences in the rank and file of the garrisons and slanderous accusations.

"I feel it my duty to bring to your attention something that I consider of grave significance to the discipline of the army, which your Excellency can easily verify if you obtain your information from those generals and commanding officers who, free from political passions, live in close contact with their subordinates and are always mindful of their intimate problems and feelings.

"Your devoted subordinate greets you most respectfully,

Francisco Franco"

Early in July he received news regarding the march of conspiracy, and the information that he, as the general most qualified, had been chosen for the command of the troops in Africa. He was also consulted upon the policy to be followed in several other places, especially in the Spanish capital.

Using a secret code, Franco wrote three letters to Madrid. In one of them he warned of the dangers of having the garrison barricade itself in the barracks, pointing out that important means and resources of the government had to be taken into account. Franco advised that the troops should concentrate in a specified place, and then fall back toward the mountains in order to join the forces advancing from the north. This letter did not accomplish its purpose, since it was not deciphered in time by the recipient.

CHAPTER XX

The Explosion

AT NOON, July 17, a telegram reached Madrid from Tetuán. It was a simple greeting from a citizen of common name and surname, signed with an even more common name. Nevertheless, it involved a sensational message. The name of the one greeted consisted of eleven letters, and that of the sender seventeen. And that message, apparently so innocuous, sent by order of Colonel Yagüe, said merely this: "The troops in Africa revolted on the sixteenth at eleven o'clock in the morning."

The events do not correspond exactly with this reference, for the army in Africa did not rise in revolt until the afternoon. But as soon as the message was received, the agents at work reported the news to the leaders of the movement which it was hoped would be Spain's salvation, to Generals Mola, Goded, and Fanjul, and to General Saliquet, who a few hours later departed for Valladolid. Through another channel the news also reached some of the leaders in the fleet, and General Queipo de Llano.

At five o'clock in the afternoon the government was already aware of the existence of untoward developments in Africa. Casares Quiroga called from the War Ministry for the Commander-General of Melilla, General Romerales, a Mason, in whom the minister had placed full confidence. What a surprise! It was not Romerales who answered the call of the minister, but rather Colonel Solans, who gave him the surprising and terrible news that Romerales could not answer the telephone because he had him in jail.

Casares Quiroga refused to believe what he heard, and to verify the incident he called up the commander of the forces in Africa, General Gómez Morato, who was in Tetuán, and who answered that he was absolutely unaware of what was happening in Melilla, but that he would verify the reports immediately. And in effect, he took an airplane to that place, where he was awaited by Legionnaires who, without the least delay, led him into the presence of Colonel Solans.

"General, we have revolted against the government for the welfare of Spain. Turn yourself over to us."

Gómez Morato did not resist but joined them.

The insurrection of the troops in Africa had been unanimous. The armies of the two zones, joined by the same ideal, had come to a common view during the maneuvers held in the middle of July on the Llano Amarillo. Lieu-tenant-Colonel Yagüe had the foresight to take along a tent, and within its canvas walls conferences and discussions were held among the leaders and officers of the forces gathered. There, garrison juntas were designated, and the manner in which the movement was to be carried out was agreed upon. The objectors were convinced, the lukewarm were encouraged, and everything was arranged and ready for the signal.

The news of the assassination of Calvo Sotelo arrived on the last night at Llano Amarillo. Among the officers there was a nephew of the ex-minister named Barber, who made ready to leave immediately for the Peninsula.

As he bid farewell to Lieutenant-Colonel Yagüe, the latter said to him, "Soon you will have news from us."

Finally the awaited order arrived. The movement was to begin on the 17th, at five o'clock in the afternoon. The troops had been prepared for that hour, but in Melilla de-velopments were premature, because General Romerales, aware of what was taking place, attempted to abort the movement by calling to his aid the revolutionary organiza-tions. There was shooting, which gave the alarm, and clashes and assaults, which were quickly checked by the Legionnaires of Lieutenant-Colonel Helio Rolando de Tella y Cantos, a leader with the name of a crusader, a model of fealty and archtype of courage, who was pursued furiously by the Republic from the very day of its establishment, and who had just arrived from the French zone, where he had taken refuge.

General Romerales was in jail, and Colonel Solans took charge of the commandancy. In Tetuán the High Commissary, Alvarez Buylla, the best example of a family of weak sisters, attempted to resist. He made incessant appeals for aid from Madrid. When he was told that the Legion and the Regulars were on their way to the High Commissariat, he submitted.

Lieutenant-Colonel Yagüe ordered from Tetuán the sending out of trucks to pick up the Fifth Banner, that of Costejón, which was in Zoco de Arbaa. At eleven thirty o'clock that night Yagüe, at the head of the Fourth Banner, which was at Dar Rifien, began the march on Ceuta, while he ordered the garrison of that city to pour out into the streets and keep the population under control, which was done without firing a single shot.

On the following day the first troops of regulars embarked for Spain. The *Churruca* transported the Oliver forces to Cádiz, and they had scarcely landed when the torpedo-boat destroyer mutinied and joined the Red squadron. Another group of soldiers under the command of Lieutenant-Colonel Amador de los Ríos left for Algeciras and disembarked at Punta Mayorga.

Red airships circled above the African troops. In the Straits, the squadron which had mutinied, was flying the flag of the revolution and attempted to prevent the passage of the troops. Franco was flying to Tetuán.

The news of the occurrences in Africa did not arouse Spain until the 18th. That morning an officious note was drawn up and sent over the air by the Union Radio which said:

"A new criminal plot against the Republic has been thwarted. The government did not wish to address the nation until it had obtained exact information about the developments and put into execution the measures necessary and urgent to combat them.

"A part of the army which represents Spain in Morocco has risen up in arms against the Republic, rebelling against the nation, and perpetrating a shameful and criminal act of rebellion against the legally constituted authority.

"The government makes known that the movement is restricted exclusively to certain cities in the zone of the Protectorate, and that no one, absolutely no one, in the Peninsula has joined in such an absurd enterprise. On the contrary the Spanish people have reacted unanimously and with profound indignation against this reprehensible attempt which was nipped in the bud.

"The government is pleased to make manifest that heroic nuclei of loyal elements have resisted the insurrection in the cities of the Protectorate, defending the honor of the soldier's uniform, the prestige of the army, and the authority of the Republic.

"At this very moment the forces of the Republic on the land and sea, and in the air, which, with the unfortunate exception designated, have remained faithful to their duty, are on their way to put down the insurrection, a stupid and shameful movement, with relentless energy.

"The government of the Republic has the situation well in hand, and affirms that it will not delay in announcing to the public that normalcy has been restored."

At three o'clock in the afternoon another report was broadcast to calm the growing anxiety:

"Again the government speaks to confirm the reports of absolute tranquillity throughout all the Peninsula.

"The government appreciates the co-operation which it has received, and in recognizing it, it insists that the best service than can be rendered to it is to guarantee normalcy in daily life in order to give a high example of serenity and confidence in the resources of the government.

"Thanks to the precautionary measures which were taken by the authorities, an extensive movement of aggression against the Republic can be considered as crushed; a movement which has found no support in the Peninsula, and which has only found a following among a small portion of the army which the Spanish Republic maintains in Morocco, and which, oblivious of its high patriotic obligations, was egged on by political passion, forgetting its most sacred promises.

"The government has been forced to take radical and urgent measures within its ranks, some already known. The others concern the detention of various generals, as well as numerous leaders and officers involved in the movement. The police have also captured a foreign airplane which, from all indications, was hired for the purpose of transporting into Spain one of the leaders of the rebellion.

"These measures, combined with the orders sent to the forces which work to thwart the rebellion in Morocco, permit us to affirm that government action will suffice to bring back normalcy."

As that afternoon drew to a close the government authorities gathered in the office of the War Ministry. Largo Caballero was called and hastened there. He not only offered the Socialist militia if needed, but also intimidated the government into arming the people without delay, for to do otherwise, he said, would stamp the ministers responsible with negligence in their duty to save the Republic.

Every hour the Radio Union sent out an officious and soothing report to repeat that the zone of the insurrection was localized in Morocco, that from end to end there was absolute tranquillity in the Peninsula, that it was untrue that a state of war had been declared, and that those that spread such reports were rebels. It was also stated that the rebels in Ceuta and Melilla had been bombarded from the air, and that units of the government squadron were advancing toward Africa. Despite the government assurances that the movement was localized, everyone knew that the events in Morocco were not a local and isolated affair, as the official reports stated.

On that same day, the 18th, General Queipo de Llano started his great feat in Seville, which he later related in the following words:

"At a quarter to two on that day, frankly no one had rebelled in Seville except Major Cuesta, my adjutant, I, . . . and a few other officers. At two o'clock two generals, two colonels, one lieutenant-colonel, and two majors were held prisoners. . . . At two thirty a state of war was proclaimed. At three o'clock many agents of the government fell into our hands as prisoners, with their weapons of combat. At five, the artillery began. At six all of the official centers were under my control. Before nightfall all of the officials of the Popular Front and all the assault guards in their service were prisoners, and the iron-clad tanks and other armaments in their possession were in our hands. At midnight the Tablada Airdrome surrendered without a shot having been fired. On the 19th Seville awoke completely Spanish, genuinely Nationalist."

On the mornings of the 18th and 19th there began to flame in many cities the fire of patriotism, which a few hours later was to rise into a gigantic conflagration which was to attract the attention of the whole world.

Desires long dormant burst forth with cries that were heartbeats, and the chains and shackles that held down the national spirit were broken. It was no longer a crime to love Spain, and these first cheers of liberation were united with sobs and tears. It was as though patriotic Spaniards had been overcome by a great fever, an organic reaction to recover, to regain their health, and to live. Those who poured out into the streets were trembling and inspired. Their eyes burned with a heroic light. Their hands trembled anxiously to grasp a rifle. Spain was shaken by an electric charge that prepared it for what was to come.

Already the bold followers of "Renovación Española," the first of Somosierra, were defending the road as one defending a treasure. It was a guerrilla war between the boldest of the bold and the Red avalanche that hammered at them from Madrid. What madness!

In Burgos the silence of the starry night was broken by the troops, a confused mass of officers, soldiers, and civilians, who passed fervently and vociferously cheering Spain.

At that moment a tremendous struggle was going on between the Nationalists and those who opposed them in most of the barracks. The pulse beat of Spain was to be found in the soldiers' rooms. Pathetic hours, loaded with responsibility and history in the making, which might give birth to a new nation.

Out of that uncertainty some of the garrisons were to come out triumphant. Others were destined for an unfortunate surrender, as was the case of the barracks of Montaña, or a sad one, as in the case of the barracks at Loyola of San Sebastián; or to succumb gloriously, as did the garrison at Barcelona and the defenders of the barracks at Simancas of Gijón, or to resist victoriously the sufferings of a long siege as was the case in Oviedo, Huesca, Teruel, and the Alcázar in Toledo. In Coruña, Avila, Cáceres, Vitoria, Zaragoza, Cádiz, Córdoba, Jaca, and a number of other places, the army rapidly gained control.

But the army was not alone. From the outset it had the effective support of the people; civilians who had hoped for this moment and who hastened to take part in the crusade. The first were the Falange and the Requetés of Valladolid, the azure city, the capital of the Spanish Falange, where the Falange was shunned, execrable, and prohibited by law, and was therefore forced to resort to clandestine activity, from which it emerged only to gamble with death, go to jail, or bury its dead. In Valladolid was organized the first division, which Colonel Serrador was to take with his troops to the heights of León, destined to be the peak of glory and suffering, the Calvary of Valladolid, and the Verdún of that hour when new frontiers were being opened for Spain.

In Pamplona, July 19 was a remarkable spectacle of the Carlist legend. Pamplona was throbbing with emotion, hoarse from cheering, her heart trembling with gratitude because the prophecies were coming true. Pamplona was red with red berets,[1] and covered with Spanish flags which were waved impatiently by those who were eager to embark upon the conquest and tell the prodigious story to the rest of the country.

A short while after four o'clock, General Mola, the outstanding leader in these developments, was reviewing the first Traditionalist battalion. Many youths who clamored outside the barracks carried the smell of the threshing floor where they had just abandoned their threshing machines. They had put on the clean shirt and the new suit which they had for the holidays. The most humble wore tattered clothes or blouses, and *alpargatas*. Some, wealthy and more haughty, did not set aside their stiff collar to become soldiers and take up a rifle, for since there were not enough uniforms for everyone, those who did not obtain them joined the battalions dressed in the clothing they happened to be wearing at the moment.

How great Navarre was on that day! In front of the barracks, where avalanches of red berets gathered, and volunteers were being enlisted for the war, the most unbelievable scenes of abnegation and patriotism were enacted. Villages like those of Mendigorría and Artajona remained not only without youths but without a single man. There were old

---

[1] Referring to the red berets worn by the Carlists, of the monarchical Carlist tradition, not to be confused with the Reds or Communists.

men who had to be held back because they wanted to rush out to the countryside to fight; the seven brothers in a family of Pamplona, rifle in hand; a father and his five sons from a village in the Rivera; a grandfather, son, and grandson in the same ranks. It was the miracle of Navarre. The miracle of Navarrese perseverance. The miracle of tradition. The aged trunk, wrinkled and nostalgic, had suddenly dressed itself in the finery of a triumphant springtime.

Evening came, and the trucks loaded with Requetés were off to war, singing old tunes with new vigor. It was as though Navarre had opened her arteries to inundate Spain to her last drop of blood. More and more trucks went forth, forming an endless line along the road, accompanied by the sound of the motors and the youthful shouting, fragrant and freedom loving, the voice of the warlike and conquering Navarre of old. And the voices vanished into the warm atmosphere of that hot July night.

Every province was at war, and within each province every city and village discussed its particular grievances. Who is capable of giving a full record of those infinite acts of heroism, performed by thousands of persons in those first days who risked their lives with as much faith as decision, some to be triumphant and others to become martyrs? Who could relate the sacrifices of the innumerable heroes, faithful to their oath and to their honor, or simply loyal to their consciences, who fulfilled their duty with no recompense other than an obscure and tragic death, offered to God and to Spain in the cellars of a Checa, within the shadows of a cemetery wall, or over a precipice from which they were flung into the sea?

Out of those first hours of chaos and confusion Spain was to emerge divided. The shining bayonets and the rattle of shots announced the new frontiers. The war had begun.

CHAPTER XXI

From Tenerife to Tetuán

SHORTLY after his arrival at Santa Cruz de Tenerife, Franco realized that he was a prisoner of the Popular Front. The political satraps who had decreed his removal from Spain had done so with another Elba in mind. But this was an Isle of Elba on which paid assassins hovered and spied on the exile as government agents. He was watched day and night, his mail was censored, his telephone messages were intercepted, and he was surrounded by a veritable ring of spies organized by the hostile authorities on the island. Hostile pens and voices assailed the general. The municipal government of Realejo Alto directed all the municipalities of the province to ask the government to dismiss Franco as a dangerous element.

A friend warned the general, "There are plans on foot to take your life."

"Two years ago," he answered, "Moscow sentenced me to death."

Round about the commandancy skulked strange persons who were seen to station themselves at strategic places. The civil guard brought the report that at a Communist meeting it had been decided to assassinate Franco, and that volunteers had offered themselves to carry out the plan. The governor knew of the plot, but as he was guaranteed very little assurance of protection, from that moment the officers of the garrison, on the initiative of the colonel of general staff, Gonzáles Peral, agreed to form a permanent personal guard to protect General Franco. Every officer, without exception, offered himself for this service, which was considered an honor. The general was unaware that he was being so carefully guarded, and of the custody in which he went on all of his trips. Even the time of his appointments was changed, without his knowledge, whenever any event was announced which he had promised to attend.

Despite these precautions, the Marxist groups did not desist in their plot to murder Franco. A plan to assassinate him at a festival in La Laguna went awry. The assassins then attempted to perpetrate the crime at the Flower Festival in Villa de Orotava. Again the attempt was frustrated.

On the night of July 13 occurred the last criminal attempt to take his life. The assassins attempted to scale the walls of the garden and from there reach the central pavilion, where Franco's sleeping quarters were located. The assailants were three. When they were climbing the wall, one of the sentinels in the garden challenged them, and as they made no response he fired on them and put them to flight. The guard stationed outside also fired, but the malefactors escaped. The civil authorities of the island hastened to the commandancy to find out what had happened. The wife and daughter of the general were also guarded by a special guard, for their lives, too, were threatened.

On July 14, the diplomat José Antonio de Sangróniz arrived at Santa Cruz de Tenerife to inform the general, with whom it was so difficult to communicate, of the latest news about the movement, and to set the date for its inauguration. The airplane which was to carry Franco to Tetuán was to arrive at Las Palmas on the following day.

"Now we must plan the escape," said the general. "I have announced, with the authorization of the ministry, an inspection tour of the islands of Fuerteventura and Lanzarote. It will be the pretext."

On the following night the general carried on long conversations with his friends concerning future developments. He had just ciphered some letters with the aid of a little book which he always had with him.

"The time is ripe," exclaimed the general, "and we cannot delay much longer, because the advances of anarchy have been considerable, and very soon they will have forestalled the possibilities of a popular reaction which still pulsates in Spain."

Someone wished to answer those words with the happy prophecy, "Within a week all will have been favorably decided."

Franco looked at him fixedly, and weighing his words, he said with a bit of severity, "If the military coup is successful, yes. But the government has many forces at its command."

There was silence until the general had completed his train of thought. He then made the prophetic statement, "If the coup fails, there will be a long and bloody civil war; the enemies of Spain are many and they are powerful."

All were silent. From the open balcony could be seen the exuberant tropical flowers, tossing in the breeze which came from over the sea. Franco rose, and to dissipate the doubts which his words had left, he added, "I have absolute faith in victory, and I am convinced that Spain, after the period of hardship which will necessarily follow that war, will recover quickly due to the recuperative faculty of the country and its people, to enter upon an era of splendor and prosperity."

On the morning of the 16th, the telegraph wires carried sad and unexpected news to Tenerife. General Amado Balmes, military commander of Las Palmas, had been killed by the bullet of a pistol which he was trying out in the target field of that city. He was the first victim of the movement, for the general had for many days been experimenting with firearms, "so that when the moment arrived the youths would be provided with a useful weapon and not something useless." Balmes was in close touch with Franco. He knew what was being planned in all its details, he was in full agreement, and was to be substitute general commandant.

Franco, saddened by the news, called the War Ministry to tell them that he planned to go to Las Palmas to attend the burial. On asking for this permission, the general turned to those who were around him, and said, "Probably they will take advantage of this occasion to dismiss me."

But that was not the case. The sub-secretary of war, in the name of the minister, authorized him to make the trip, and at twelve thirty o'clock that night General Franco, with his wife and daughter, embarked on the inter-insular ship *Viera y Clavijo*. His adjutants accompanied him, four officers as guards, two infantrymen and two artillerymen, and the fiscal judge, Martínez Fusset.

All of the officers of the garrison and many other private citizens were at the pier. The general carried as his only baggage a small valise which contained a black suit. The siren screamed long and loudly and the farewells began. Franco, without showing the emotion that ran through his soul, embraced his companions with words of encouragement and confidence. Colonel Gonzáles Peral was the last one to see him off.

"God be with you, my general," he said.

"I hope so," answered Franco.

The boat glided out into the Atlantic night. Very soon the point where sky and sea met was a diadem of glimmering lights in infinity, surrounded by shadows. The people on the pier still had their eyes fixed on that constellation of rubies which soon vanished from sight. There went Franco, their great hope, to his destiny.

Immediately following the burial of General Balmes, at noon on the 17th, Franco spent all his time receiving calls at his hotel, where he virtually incarcerated himself. At three o'clock in the morning the adjutants and guarding officers were awakened abruptly by the fiscal judge Martínez Fusset, who brought sensational news.

"The troops in Africa have rebelled," he said, "we must take extreme precautions."

All put on their clothing without delay and went out into the hallway, where Franco soon appeared, for he already knew what was happening, having been informed at two fifteen by the commandant at Tenerife. He was dressed in civilian clothes and carried a valise in his hand. He climbed into the carriage which awaited him and went to the commandancy. In the staff offices he donned his military uniform. At this moment General Orgaz arrived, the first in the uprising, since 1931, and took over control of the civil government at seven o'clock that morning. The commandancy immediately gained new courage. Officers came and went, orders were drawn up and the telephones rang continuously. The axis of Spain passed through the office at Las Palmas at that time. Franco drew up a manifesto and dictated the first orders as the "Rebel" leader to assure the triumph of the movement in the Canaries. He remained in the commandancy until eleven o'clock when he went out to find an airplane that awaited him, where again there were farewells and applause for the leader.

The general repeated his watchword, "Blind faith in victory!"

An automobile carried him to the pier where he was awaited by the tugboat which was to take him to the airdrome at Gaudo. There was a moment of delay, while Franco said good-by to his wife and daughter.

"Tell them," he told one of his officers, "that I have gone to make an inspection and that I will see them soon."

Franco was dressed in mourning. He was well shaven. He had disposed of his mustache. He wore glasses and carried a diplomatic passport in his pocket. He had to provide for any contingency at the ports of Agadir and Casablanca.

At the Gaudo airdrome a mysterious six-passenger bi-motor plane, the *O — H — Rapide,* had been awaiting him since the 15th. It had arrived from Croydon with some English tourists. These were Major Hugo B. C. Pollard, an expert in handling weapons from Scotland Yard, his daughter Diana, a beautiful blonde girl of nineteen years, and her friend Dorothy Watson, also young and beautiful.

How and why had they gone to Las Palmas? Since it had been decided that Franco would travel by air to Tetuán, the author Luis A. Bolin, who resided in London, had been chosen to rent a fast airplane. The author obtained one from the Olley Aircraft Company, and invited his friend Mr. Pollard to go on the mission with his daughter and a friend of hers in the guise of tourists, to free from all suspicion the presence of an airplane in Las Palmas. The craft was to be piloted by Captain Beed, an expert pilot who had made many famous flights.

"Are you willing to undertake a flight to the Canaries?" Bolin had asked him. "It must be with the express understanding that there will be no landing in Spanish territory for any reason whatever. And once in Las Palmas, you will pick up a 'certain person' to carry him to Tetuán."

The captain accepted the proposition. On the 11th they left Croydon in London. There were stops at Bordeaux and Oporto to take on gasoline. There was another landing at Casablanca, where Bolin remained to await the return, for he was to accompany General Franco on his flight to Tetuán. And finally, they reached Las Palmas. There, the pilot, the mechanic, and the English travelers, unaware of what was taking place, were surprised and nervous. Captain Beed has described those days of mystery and uncertainty as he witnessed them.

"When I was in my hotel room the day after my

arrival," he relates, "I stretched out in my bed to take a siesta, when I heard soft knocks at my door.

" 'Come in,' I cried.

"The visitor, a stranger to me, excused himself for the intrusion, and began an endless barrage of questions. He wanted to know the purpose of my trip to Las Palmas without carrying the customary papers, who I was and with whom I had made the trip. I merely answered that I was an airplane pilot in the service of some tourists, and that I was piloting a rented craft. And when the conversation was concluded, the unknown visitor told me in a low voice, 'The general wishes to see you.'

" 'What general?' I answered.

" 'Quiet!' he said.

"And without further explanations, he asked this last question, 'Do you know where the church is?'

"The church? I know where the cathedral is located."

" 'Very well, that is sufficient,' he continued. 'At four o'clock sharp you must be near the main entrance. A carriage will stop for you and the coachman will make a signal. Climb into the vehicle immediately and it will take you into the mountains.' "

(These and other confidential questions put to the pilot were made because those at Las Palmas who were involved, not having received an exact description of the characteristics of the airplane, did not know with certainty whether or not the one which had just arrived was the one rented to pick up General Franco, and they were investigating in order to make sure.)

"A short while later," continued Captain Beed, "I was presented to General Orgaz, who also began to question me, repeating questions similar to those asked of me at the hotel. He finished by confiding to me that 'a certain person' was awaiting the arrival of an English aviator and this aviator must be 'myself.'

"I was completely in the dark. But this was not all, for

I had scarcely left General Orgaz when another Spaniard came up to me and gave me to understand, in so many words, that I should best forget the whole incident and not think about it again.

" 'The whole incident? I must say that it would be difficult for me to reconstruct in entirety what had taken place. We shall see what is going to happen,' I told myself.

"That night and on the following morning I was undisturbed, but in the afternoon the ceremony was repeated. At about four o'clock a new messenger came to visit me. He spoke English perfectly. Was I dealing with a fellow citizen? No. Never have I seen a more pure Castilian type. After greeting me in a friendly manner, he begged me to follow him out to the terrace, where, after making sure that no one was in the vicinity, he read to me from a slip of paper which carried the following order, 'Lead him to a certain person.'

"Finally I was to discover the enigma. I was about to really meet the person who held all the threads of this intrigue. But at the last minute the orders were countermanded, and it was decided that I should go to the mountains, where I was to remain hidden until my passenger would be ready to undertake the journey.

"On the following day I began to see light. The Spanish visitor of the night previous came to see me at four o'clock in the morning, and showing signs of excitement, he told me that the moment was at hand. Nothing was said about going to the mountains. The plot was about to be unraveled. I would soon know everything. I dressed hurriedly and followed the stranger to a near-by room. There I waited until eleven fifty-five a.m., when I was notified to be in readiness. At twelve o'clock sharp I received a second order, this time shorter and more imperative, 'We must go!'

"Escorted by a detachment of armed motorcycles, I was taken to the airdrome. The automobile traveled at full speed, only slowing up at designated places, where emissaries sent ahead to spy out the land reported to us with rapid gestures that the road was clear. I saw my airplane in the middle of the field, ready for the take-off.

"'Are the tanks full?' I asked.

"'Everything is in readiness,' answered a mechanic.

"'And the passenger?'

"'There he is.'"

On the near-by shore a tugboat tossed about on the water, and its passengers were carried ashore on the shoulders of the sailors. One of them, more determined than the others, walked ahead, approached the pilot, and stretching out his hand, said to him, "I am General Franco."

The motors began to roar. The general bid farewell, one by one, to those who surrounded him. Their eyes gleamed with hope, and they were pale with emotion. The general, serene, repeated his counsels. With him embarked the military aviator Villalobos and his adjutant Franco Salgado. The airplane sped down the runway and was soon in the air. It disappeared in the distant blue of the sky. It was exactly two ten p.m., July 18, 1936, a moment memorable in Spanish history.

After a short stop in Agadir, the plane continued on to Casablanca, where it landed at nine thirty p.m. There Bolin was waiting, having exercised his patience for four days awaiting this airplane loaded with hopes and an imponderable treasure of high expectations. From the airdrome the travelers went to a small hotel in the vicinity, where, after eating, they engaged in a conversation which was carried on almost entirely by General Franco, who discussed the subject which was nearest to his heart, abounding with hope, Spain and its future. During those hours of the night and early morning, meaningful hours for the future of Spain, he gave every promise of desiring good government. It was three o'clock in the morning and Franco gave no thought to sleep.

"General," reminded Bolin, "think of the day of excitement and work which awaits you."

"Well, it is too late to sleep now," was his answer.

"Then what?" continued Bolin.

"I am going to bathe," was the answer.

At four o'clock in the morning they left for the airdrome, and a half hour later they were again in the air. Sunrise found them over the Beni-Arós mountains, brightened by blending rose-colored and golden hues. Franco recognized by name the roughest parts of the mountains, the steep cliffs, and the crests. The sky was radiant. At seven o'clock that morning Tetuán loomed in the distance, dazzling in the rays of the sun. Tetuán! The airdrome was swarming with people. The plane circled low and Franco recognized friends. Finally they landed. The motor still roared, and there was cheering and applause. Franco emerged smiling. Lieutenant-Colonel Yagüe was at the side of the plane. Legionnaires rendered homage.

At the offices of the High Commissary there gathered the leaders and officers of the Regular Army, of the Legion, and of the *mejalas*, the men who soon were to stir Spain with their valor, heroes who wept on hearing Franco's voice, a voice that already appeared to have been silenced by exile, to be forgotten forever. It was the voice of Spain; voice from her heart and steeped in the nation's past.

"We were coming to a point," said Franco, "when we were ashamed of being Spaniards and of wearing our uniforms, which represented our honor, our pride, and our spiritual patrimony! Now we are on our way. Each one to his post, to fulfill his duty. For Spain everything we may do will seem very little. The offering of our lives for its cause is a glorious deed if the nation will have reconquered its soul and its glory, and will have come to see itself face to face again."

The officers listened with stout hearts, their muscles

quivering, and tears in their eyes. Their emotion finally burst forth in cheering and applause. From there, the general went to address the Banners of the Legion formed in Dar Rifien.

Just as he was leaving, an officer notified him, "My general, some suspicious ships are cruising in the vicinity of Ceuta and they do not answer to the signals which are made to them."

"Have them repeated," Franco ordered, "and if they do not answer, fire on them."

During the night the voice of Franco, a victorious voice, reached Spain from end to end through the miracle of radio:

"On taking over the command of this glorious and patriotic army here in Tetuán, I send to the loyal garrisons and their country the most enthusiastic greetings. Spain has been saved. You may pride yourselves on being Spaniards.

"Have blind faith. Never doubt. Gather energy, without pausing, for the nation demands it. The movement is marching on. There is no human force which will stop it. I greet you with a strong and hearty embrace. Long live Spain!"

Franco then prepared to spend his third sleepless night devoted to hard work.

When the first news of the military uprising in Morocco reached Madrid, Azaña, President of the Republic, felt the same uneasiness that he had experienced on that morning of August 10, 1932, the occasion of General Sanjurjo's insurrection. Just as he had then called upon the governor of Coruña, now he asked insistently, "What is Franco doing?"

In his desire to calm the nerves of the president, Casares Quiroga answered, "He is well guarded on the Canary Islands."

CHAPTER XXII

The Battle of the Straits

THE news that reached Franco during his first days at Tetuán was not good news. Hopes and expectations seemed to be crumbling into failure. The navy, already Red, blocked the passage across the Straits for the army. Spain offered a picture of confusion, which each day assumed a more tragic aspect. The army of the north lacked material, ammunition, and the most essential necessities for war. Red emissaries were shouting the victory of the "loyal forces" in Madrid, Vizcaya, Guipúzcoa, Santander, Levante, and Catalonia. The entire southern part of Spain was aflame, and Queipo de Llano, with very little equipment, had to be everywhere at the same time in order to be on hand where voices called for help, while he maintained himself with genial improvisations in Seville, which was dominated by the Reds and which the revolution looked upon as its own.

The insurgent movement had against it the navy and the greater part of the diplomatic corps, and the gold in the country was in the possession of the government at Madrid, as were also the best artillery armories and the armaments of entire divisions which were in the Marxist zone. And the attempts on the part of insurgents were a series of misfortunes. First there was the death of Sanjurjo, then the *Churruca* got away, the garrison at Barcelona was lost after a struggle, and the greater part of the air forces were loyal to the government. Traditionalist Spain fixed its eyes and its hopes upon General

Franco, who had to cut his way through the thickness of adversity and misfortunes.

"Never," relates one of his close friends, "did we see the general more the master of himself than at that time. Far from giving way under the weight of misfortunes which were added to each day, he stood defiant. He contemplated with indifference and without being perturbed the chasms of catastrophe that opened up at his very feet."

Franco's fortitude appeared to make him seemingly invincible. He continued to receive disconcerting messages, some by radio, others mysterious messages in code which he personally deciphered. There were messages from Mola, Queipo de Llano, and Aranda. Franco devoured these tragic messages in silence, without a spark of that forge which was burning within him ever becoming visible on his countenance. To those who were about him, impatient to know, he simply said, "Good news."

And he continued his work. Not once did the report of an adversity interrupt or slow up his labor. To a failure here or there, he would answer immediately with a plan. If one front collapsed he would establish another. His mind provided for every contingency.

"The troops cannot cross the Straits," he was told.

"They will cross by air," was his answer.

And so he began to organize an air transport company, for other nations agreed only to sell him commercial planes. Ten days later there arrived at Tetuán the first two airplanes, capable of transporting twenty-five men each.

One day, toward the end of July, the ships that belonged to the fleet began to congregate in the waters off Tangier. They arrived separately, and by different routes, by order of the Ministry of Marine in Madrid. Those ships gathered there no longer formed the Spanish Armada. They were now something different; they were the Red fleet. On their decks the splendid seamen of former days had been transformed into hordes who raised their blood-stained fists, for they had killed their officers, fulfilling the orders of the Ministry of Marine. The crews were little more than groups of assassins, surprised to see themselves at liberty and in possession of ships that traveled the seas, loaded with ignominy, like those fantastic ships of legend, carrying mutinous or pirate crews.

More ships continued to congregate. There were cruisers, torpedo boats, torpedo-boat destroyers, gunboats, revenue cutters, and auxiliary vessels. The arrival of each one of them marked a new and unfortunate chapter in the drama of the Spanish Armada. It was always the same scene of terror and bloodshed. The officers were either hung, or placed in the holds, or delivered over to the mob, or to the fury of a popular tribunal in a Red port.

On the 20th, toward evening, the curls of smoke from a large vessel could be perceived on the horizon. It was the ironclad ship *Jaime I,* escorted by the cruisers *Miguel de Cervantes* and *Libertad,* which had gone out to meet it. It was a giant with its entrails rent apart. It was a floating castle in which some heroes, having taken refuge on the bridge, surrounded by the vastness of the ocean, were confronted by a mutinous crew which from that moment became "the glorious crew," which Giral, at that time at the head of the government, congratulated enthusiastically, also ordering that the dead be dropped into the sea "with respectful solemnity." And with the arrival of the *Jaime I* the Red fleet at Tangier was completed, ready now to carry on its operations. "The fleet is ours," cried Indalecio Prieto over a microphone in Madrid that night. Other radios repeated the news immediately. Masters of the fleet, the African troops in the zone of the Protectorate were rendered powerless, and the insurgents in Spain lost their best source of aid.

On the following day the ships began to bombard a few places on the Spanish coast which were under the control of the army. The work done, they would return to Tangier where they took on supplies, while their crews fraternized with the revolutionary elements of the city where incursions into Spanish Morocco were being plotted. It was at this time that the Commission of the International Zone received a condemnatory note from General Franco, in which he denounced the powers signatory to the Statute of having violated the neutrality therein pacted, by favoring a belligerent. And if the violation continued, the general "reserved the right to use Tangier to his best advantage for the cause of Spain, which was what he defended." The arrival of the note was accompanied by the sound of arms. Soldiers were sent to the boundary line between Spanish Morocco and the Tangier zone. The city spent several hours of anxiety, fearing the outbreak of guerrilla warfare in their streets, led by the Legionnaires.

Immediately warships of all the powers signatory to the Statute gathered in the bay of Tangier, and landed Marine contingents to protect the neutrality of the zone. General Franco pointed out in a second note the reasons which forbade the Red ships from remaining in Tangier. He considered them ships which should be looked upon as piratical, since their officers had been assassinated. They were obtaining supplies in a neutral port, and their crews were attempting to arm certain Spaniards in Tangier for the purpose of using them to attack Tetuán and Ceuta, all of which were a transgression of the international treaties which protected the neutrality of Tangier.

On the receipt of these notes, the Committee for Control of the International Zone notified the Madrid government, charged it as responsible for this delicate situation, and urged it to order the withdrawal of the ships from Tangier without delay, or else "they will be obliged to consider themselves prisoners of the French, English, Italian, and Portuguese squadrons which are now stationed in that port."

On July 23, in the night, the Red ships abandoned Tangier. The president of the Committee for Control now traveled to Tetuán to urge Franco to withdraw his troops from the border. The general answered that he was willing to respect the rights established, but he demanded that all should respect them on an equal basis.

Still, on several occasions Red submarines and torpedo boats returned to Tangier to take shelter. Franco's protest was followed up. He continued to concentrate troops on the border. Meanwhile, he denounced the Commander-General of Gibraltar, stating that pirate ships were being provided with supplies and food there. On August 6, Red ships again appeared off Tangier. General Franco answered with a protest which was the equivalent of an ultimatum. The International Commission demanded of the Madrid government the immediate departure of the squadron. That same night the ships abandoned Tangier definitely, and the Spanish troops withdrew from the border.

With the battle of the Straits, General Franco won a victory essential for the development of his war program. Master of Africa, and master of the Straits, the army, from a strictly international aspect, was no longer in rebellion but had virtually assumed belligerent status.

When Morocco was definitely a part of the movement Franco had in his hands a formidable weapon, because the possession of Morocco and the Straits was vital for his cause. Through that zone Franco obtained international status. Morocco and the Straits were his contacts with foreign powers. Algeciras and Ceuta bordered on English territory, and Tangier meant contact with the nations signatory to the Statute. These nations could neither overlook the fact that the Tangier area and the shores of the Straits were in the possession of those whom the Madrid government branded as rebels, nor that in reality they controlled these areas without risk of loss and with indisputable authority. These facts not only had to be recognized but also respected.

Nothing could have been more disastrous to the Reds

than these developments. From Azaña to Alvarez del Vayo, passing through all the Red leaders of the government, plans were sought to crush Franco's success, and in their despair they offered interested nations the occasion to gather in Morocco on the pretext that sovereignty there resided in the Sultan, and by his delegation "in the legitimate Spanish government." No nation dared to become a party to such a plan, nor even to place the disputed area within reach of its grasp.

The Madrid government then attempted to stir up the Moroccan tribes. They were stirred up over the radio with rabid speeches in Arabic, undesirables were bribed, and agents were sent out to foment insurrection. It was all in vain. Morocco remained loyal to the army. The Moors reverenced Franco, whose military prowess overpowered them. They called him "The Victorious," "Chief of Chiefs," "The Sacred One," and "Bold as the Lion."

But there were still other means of persuasion. Red warships and airplanes attempted to obtain control through methods of warfare. The squadron bombarded Ceuta, and the airplanes bombed the large mezquita of Tetuán. The Moors, incited, poured out into the streets clamoring for weapons to combat the enemy. The Grand Vizier calmed and convinced them.

"General Franco," he told them, "great and noble by the will of God, knows that he can rely upon our hearts and strength. General Franco is with us."

Although the transportation of troops and war materials continued, including complete batteries, in airplanes that terrorized Seville and Jeréz, and an occasional risky passage of Legionnaires in feluccas, General Franco considered it possible to transport the major portion by water. And, in effect, he planned to organize a convoy protected by the gunboat *Dato* and a detachment of airplanes.

He submitted the project to the study and advice of some military leaders and naval experts, who rejected it from the very beginning, deeming it unfeasible. To defy the Red fleet with a few merchant ships escorted by a gunboat, appeared to them to be a rash act with little possibility of success and which might cost them dearly.

But the general insisted and argued his plan, rejecting the objections of the leaders and experts as inacceptable and inexact, on the grounds that they reasoned from false premises; namely, that they conceded to the Red fleet the power and effectiveness of a fleet under normal conditions, calculating on the basis of tonnage and cannons, whereas, in Franco's opinion, those ships without officers or a regulated command were mere shadows, and their offensive power was only in outward appearance, lacking effectiveness.

He defended his project with such earnest determination that he succeeded in carrying it out. As a result preparations were made for the convoy, which was to be one of the most brilliant feats of the war. The convoy left Ceuta in the early afternoon of August 5. It consisted of five trans-Mediterranean ships carrying three thousand men, Regulars and Legionnaires, two batteries, two million cartridges, twelve tons of dynamite, and three thousand cannon shells.

The ships wormed their way, and their progress was followed with the greatest curiosity, for everyone knew the great risk involved in the voyage and how much was at stake for the future success of the war. The first half of the crossing was made without mishap, but a short while later a torpedo-boat destroyer was sighted bearing down upon the convoy. It was the *Alcalá Galiano*.

The *Dato* went out to meet it, and as soon as they were within firing distance both opened cannon fire, and they were in the midst of combat, in which one of the transports, which was armed, also participated. Regulars and Legionnaires, under cover, rifle in hand, asked permission to board and take possession of the ship. But the Red destroyer was held off at a great distance by the *Dato*, which, having shorter range cannons, was forced to enter within the firing zone, advancing decidedly toward the Red ship, which it attacked with unparalleled heroism, officers and sailors rivaling each other in bravery and indifference toward death.

The struggle was at its height when four airplanes from Seville made their appearance overhead, and began to circle above the *Alcalá Galiano,* which immediately veered around and took to flight at a velocity of thirty knots an hour, "their conduct contrasting with that of the *Dato,*" according to the official report, "whose commander, Don Manuel Súnico, conducted himself admirably, for the *Alcalá Galiano* could have sunk all the ships without impunity, which did not occur, fortunately, for lack of skill and due to excessive fear."

The convoy entered Tarifa without mishap, to the great joy of the Spanish people there. Franco could not conceal his satisfaction over the fact that his predictions had been fulfilled to the letter.

"It is the triumph of faith and discipline. Divine Providence is with us," he exclaimed.

General Franco reported the event to the authorities at the Naval Base at El Ferrol with the following wireless message:

"Yesterday we completed the operation in the Straits, beating off the squadron, and we reached Algeciras with a convoy of five ships with supplies and troops, accompanied by air and naval action, a gunboat, the *Dato,* a torpedo boat, the *19,* and a *Uad.* The action in the air was admirable and effective, clearing the way for us. But when we reached English waters a destroyer, which was pursued by airplanes, delayed our passage. The destroyer landed 18 dead and 28 seriously wounded at Gibraltar, the work of our hydroplanes. We succeeded in having the governor of Gibraltar oblige them to take to sea. Other ships of the squadron arrived, but they were put to flight by our airplanes which made many direct hits. The destroyer *Lazaga* went to the aid of the enemy ships. The rest were routed handily. There was another attempt to attack us, and the gunboat *Dato* put the enemy to flight. The squadron had many casualties, with many dead and wounded. On our part we did not have a single casualty nor was there any damage done to our supplies. In the landing, the gunboat *Dato*, the torpedo boat *19*, the *Uad-K. R.*, and the *T.*, participated brilliantly. They fought with great enthusiasm and effectiveness, as did also the navy hydroplanes, which made many direct hits on the destroyers, all of them effective. Long live the Spanish Navy!"

Other convoys were to follow this one which had crossed the Straits with such singular good fortune. The crossing at Gibraltar was in the hands of the Nationalists. The Red squadron was now no more than a handful of useless ships, hidden, like dragons without claws or teeth, in the caves of the Mediterranean.

A few days later General Franco crossed also, along with his troops, which, organized in columns, began the conquest of Extremadura (southwestern Spain), and began to open the way to Madrid.

CHAPTER XXIII

Franco in Cáceres

HAVING pacified the province of Seville, conquered Mérida, and opened the breach of Badajoz, the Army of the South went up toward the Tajo line, in glorious marches under a burning August sun.

The Army of the South was an impetuous array of Moors and Legionnaires led by the best captains of the Spanish army — Varela, Yagüe, Asensio, Castejón, El Mizzian, Barrón, Serrano — who traveled over parched fields enveloped in clouds of dust and gunpowder smoke. Besides the fire of those dogdays they withstood the fire of combat, leaving behind them a red trail, the price of heroism, on the dry and yellow fields of Extremadura and Toledo.

Franco, Commander-in-Chief of the Army of Africa and southern Spain, in order to lead his troops at close range, abandoned the palace of Yanduri, in Seville, where he had his general headquarters, and traveled by airplane to Cáceres on the afternoon of August 26, 1936, installing himself in the Palace of the Golfines de Arriba, the most ample of all those in the ancient city. The palace had thick, fortified walls, characteristic of a medieval edifice, with its battlements and towers, its loopholes and cisterns, and which today, restored and redecorated in the interior to meet the modern needs of its present owner, Don Gonzalo López Montenegro y Carvajal, has not lost any of its nobility, splendor, or ancient atmosphere.

The palace is in the San Mateo district, where are located the old mansions of gilded stone, sturdy as fortresses and adorned with heraldic figures. From the spacious entrance way, with its large lantern, one passes, to the left, on the ground floor, into four successive rooms, arranged in Spanish style, with dark socles and the walls covered with red damask.

The general headquarters were established in these rooms almost overnight, and it was not long before the quietness of the house was ended. It now vibrated as though it were the nerve center of the whole war. The political headquarters and the adjutants' quarters were established next to the office of the general, where telephones were installed. Three radio stations, set up with remarkable speed, completed the lines of communication. In a room next to the general's office there were stands upon which were mounted enormous maps and topographical charts, upon which were focused the strong lights of several projectors. Six other offices were being arranged for the officers of the General Staff. From the moment that Franco arrived, the house seemed to vibrate with activity, and there was no moment of rest, day or night.

General Franco's office was a small room, with a high ceiling, and the floors of polished red brick with helmets and lions in green and white. In front of the table stood an ordinary sort of chair lined in black leather. To the right was a library, which led off at an angle. To the left was a large window grated with iron bars, through which one could see a wall of blackish stone, covered with ivy. The mantels were full of pictures, including a framed genealogical chart. There was also a jewel box. Upon the table of Spanish design, papers were piled high, held down by pieces of minerals, and there was a lamp with a purple shade.

At eight o'clock in the morning the general entered his office. He ate at three, three thirty, or four o'clock depending upon the urgency of the work at hand. At five o'clock he resumed his work, which sometimes lasted until three or four o'clock in the morning, with a short interruption for dinner.

Franco spent long and endless hours of study and meditation over his maps and charts, working out the secrets of their topographical details and annotations. He worked out arithmetical and geometric problems, and re-enacted in his mind many battles as though they were taking place on those stands before his very eyes. He followed with such exactness the details of the war, that he knew to the minute where the resistance of the enemy was most tenacious and dangerous.

He knew the importance of all of the elements of warfare, and both the advantages and the weaknesses of his own forces. And so he would make such annotations as these: "That battery is not well situated. It cannot hold out there. Transfer it to the protection of that hillock which is six hundred meters to the right."

In his office, with the valuable collaboration of the General Staff, the objectives of each operation were studied, the movements of the advancing troops were co-ordinated, efforts were made to combine the effective action of the artillery forces with that of the air force, sites were chosen for the placement of reserves, and a close record was kept of the amount of ammunition which was being used up. General Franco was directing the Army of the South, but he was also in close touch with developments on the entire battle front, which extended roughly from north to south over the full length of Spain, a distance of approximately three thousand kilometers.

At evening came the balance of the day's accomplishments. Franco's first interest was to find out how many casualties there were. His facial expression reflected the impression the answer made upon him. This balancing of events resulted either in warm congratulations or the most severe reprimands. And the general never forgot about his soldiers. He was interested in the needs of the wounded, and was eager to learn of any acts of bravery and reports commending the heroism of his troops. And frequently, while listening, his eyes would become moist.

One day his press chief, Mr. Bolin, recounted to the general an episode which occurred in one of the hospitals on the front. He had entered one of the rooms where a number of Legionnaires were lying on cots, and a lieutenant of the Legion who was among them, and who had been seriously wounded, had a high fever and was delirious. The officer, in his delirium, thought that he was on the firing line, in the full heat of battle, and he was haranguing the Legionnaires with stirring words, fired by his fever, urging them on to the attack. His harangue resounded throughout the room, and everyone listened in silence to his voice which was impregnated with war nostalgia, a voice which permeated the room like the fiery breath of combat, disturbed up to that time only by the tremor of sighs and muffled exclamations of unhappiness. Suddenly he stopped talking, and all that could be heard was his panting and the rattle in his throat.

But in a few moments he regained strength and suddenly cried out in a heart-rending and tragic voice, "Come here Legion! Come here Legion!"

Upon hearing this call all the Legionnaires who were in their cots gathered as if by a mysterious and superhuman force, some leaving their beds with painful difficulty, in order to go to the bedside of their comrade, who, in agony, continued to cry out, "Come here Legion! Come here Legion!"

The Legionnaires gathered as though by the force of a magnet. Some were limping, or on crutches, or with their arms in slings, or with their heads bandaged. Others were flushed with fever, or pale and unsteady. But all answered to the implacable command, and the nuns and nurses could not hold them back despite the fact that they insisted that he was delirious and did not know what he was saying.

They merely answered, "He is calling us. He is calling us."

And the Legionnaires, the martyred Legion, as a guard of honor and loyalty, surrounded the bed where the officer, panting and convulsive, soon lay motionless forever.

When Bolín finished his account tears came to General Franco's eyes. "Have the names of that officer and those Legionnaires verified," he said.

Franco spent several weeks in Cáceres without going out into the street once. His life was limited to his office, near telephones and maps. On Sundays he attended Mass in the chapel of the house. Frequently he would check the latest reports from the battle front. A few hours in the afternoon he spent visiting generals and commanding officers, who reported news concerning their troops, aviators who reported the investigations made on their flights, and diplomats and foreign news correspondents.

On September 23, a very welcome surprise awaited him. Doña Carmen Polo, the wife of the general, arrived at Cáceres from the Canary Islands. When she arrived at the palace Franco was presiding over a meeting of commanding officers. His wife had to wait over an hour before seeing him. War demanded its tyrannical privileges.

On September 25, in the afternoon, the general said to his General Staff, "Tomorrow we will enter Toledo and rescue the defenders of the Alcázar."

The prophecy of Colonel Moscardó was about to be fulfilled. In his *Diario de operaciones* the colonel had written:

"July 21. During the night General Riquelme called me up from Toledo asking me to surrender, asking me what motivated the position I persisted in maintaining. I answered him that above all it was the love for Spain, which was in danger of falling into the hands of the Marxists, that it would be a dishonorable and shameless order which would surrender to the Red forces the armaments of the cadets, and our blind confidence in General Franco."

On August 23, an airplane carried a message of greeting

from Franco's army to the besieged, urging them to keep up their resistance. The general had in mind from the very beginning the relief of the besieged Alcázar, and sensed the epic which was being unfolded in its subterranean passages, which he knew so well.

The night of the 26th was spent in conference with Varela. The Sixth Banner of the Legion had taken possession of Bargas. The forces were in a position to enter Toledo. And on the following day, Sunday, September 27, the Legionnaires of the Fifth Banner, under the command of Tiede Zedem, and the Regulars of Del Oro, won for Nationalist Spain the imperial city, and the defenders of the Alcázar poured out from the débris free and unconquered.

General Franco greeted the heroes. On the morning of the 29th, he climbed the pile of ruins under which there were still many hand grenades and cannon shells which had not exploded, like a pilgrim climbing a sacred mountain which still stood through faith in an ideal and sacrifices superior to all the efforts to destroy it. Through that road covered over with débris, he reached the desolate patio where he was awaited by Colonel Moscardó, the dynamo of the resistance and the moving spirit behind those ruins; the true hero of the Alcázar. Moscardó, tall, stern, his beard unkempt, showed emaciation from fatigue and great hardship.

"My general," he said to Franco, "I turn over to you the Alcázar, demolished but still honorable."

"I have never had a greater ambition," he answered, "than to liberate the Alcázar."

In the patio stood the invincible legion: officers and soldiers, cadets, civil guards, assault guards, special guards, and civilians, all of them battered, dirty, disheveled, and tired, their eyes burning with fever. Groups of women and children, thin and emaciated, crowded the corridors; these were the inhabitants of those catacombs where they had spent the two most dramatic months of their lives.

In that scene, formerly one of horror and now one of victory, with its broken columns, twisted iron, and crushed stone, Moscardó spoke again to say, "We took an oath to give up our lives for our country before surrendering, and we have been faithful to our promise. With our thoughts on Spain, on our glorious traditions, and on the example of our heroes, we were honorable to our pledge, fulfilling our duty."

The voice of Moscardó, calm and firm, showed no hesitation or alteration. When he finished his speech Franco embraced him with great emotion. Then the general spoke:

"Heroes of the Alcázar! Your example will live throughout the centuries, because you have been able to uphold with your bravery the glories of the Empire through which you became strong.

"The nation owes eternal acknowledgment to all of you. The book of history is too small for the greatness of your deeds. You have exalted your people and you have raised Spain to new heights, giving it unfading glory. I greet you and embrace you in the name of our country, and I bring to you its gratitude and its recognition of your heroism; and I wish to announce that as a reward for your sacrifice the Laureate has been conferred upon you, upon Colonel Moscardó personally, and collectively upon all the defenders. Long live Spain!"

Shouting broke out, strange though it sounded, and those men, invulnerable to emotion, tried in all kinds of adversity, felt the tears of joy swelling in their eyes. And in response they cheered the general. In the sky above, three Nationalist airplanes circled over the Alcázar as a token of homage, gleaming under the golden rays of that autumn morning.

A staff correspondent of the London *Daily Express,* a newspaperman adept at waxing eloquent, wrote that it was the most dramatic scene that he had ever witnessed. Those human specters, half starved, holding weapons that were no longer of any use. They had nothing. They had to learn how to live all over again, and they had not yet decided to leave the scene of their martyrdom. Then they saw Franco. Many of them did not know him, but upon hearing the cry "General Franco!" those people began to come to life again, as though they had been revived by some device. The name of Franco meant everything to them, and they were united in their feelings. It was the name which they had awaited as they resisted. They cried out in shrill tones to express their diverse sentiments. They cheered, wept, and embraced the soldiers. It was an unforgettable spectacle in which it seemed that some had lost their minds completely.

When Franco left the Alcázar to reconnoiter the city, he was bid farewell with loud cheers from the heroes who remained there.

CHAPTER XXIV

Generalissimo Francisco Franco

.

"EVERY reason," read the decree of the National Defense Council of September 29, 1936, "points to the convenience of concentrating in one person all those powers which will lead to a final victory, and to the establishment, consolidation, and development of the new State, with the loyal assistance of the Nation. An organic and efficient regime has been established, in effect, which may answer adequately to the realities of present-day Spain, and may plan its future with absolute authority."

And so, His Excellency, Division General Francisco Franco Baamonde, was named as the head of the Nationalist government, "who shall assume all of the powers of the new State." Article II of this decree also named him "Generalissimo of the national forces of land, sea, and air."

The Generalissimo and head of the government of Nationalist Spain was now installed in the Episcopal Palace at Salamanca. From that vantage point he could envision with clear detail the whole national scene, and there he felt the full weight of growing responsibilities.

A temporary war-time government, of necessity highly centralized, was in operation from the beginning of the Civil War. The Technical Junta of the State, to give its official name, insured peace and order behind the lines, and provided all the means essential for the care and provisioning of the army at the front. Its jurisdiction extended from the complexities of trade and industry to the more subtle

social and cultural problems. Most of the Nationalist activities were under the control of the Junta with the exception
of diplomacy, which was under the Secretary of Foreign
Relations, the army, and public order, which came under
the jurisdiction of the Interior Police. The Junta was housed
in an old palace in Burgos.

The efficiency of the Junta was primarily due to the fact
that it was formed by a group of technical experts. The
Junta was made up of six commissions, each an equivalent
of one of the old Ministries. At the head of these was an
executive department headed by General Gomez Jordana,
which resembled the old office of the Head of the Cabinet.
The commissions were as follows: Finance, Industry and
Commerce, Culture, Justice, Public Works and Communications, Labor. Each commission included five men and a
president. Each president in his turn was under the absolute jurisdiction of the President of the Junta.

By the decree of September 29, 1936, General Franco was
vested with absolute civil and military authority. However,
the basic structure of the government remained unchanged.
It was a war measure. To quote Franco: "The implanting
of the most severe principles of authority which this movement implies, is not exclusively military in character, rather
it is the establishment of a hierarchical regime, through the
harmonious functioning of which all the powers and ener-
gies of the Nation will develop. . . . When the new Spanish
State becomes stronger and its development becomes more
normal, it will advance further toward the decentralization
of those functions which are not essential, and every region,
municipality, association, and individual will enjoy more
ample liberties, within the supreme interest of the State."

Meanwhile, the Civil War continued. Out of the 195,207
square miles which constitute the Spanish territory, the
Nationalist forces now occupied 108,157 square miles. The
twenty-eight provinces which that area represented, contained 11,575,289 inhabitants. By the end of the year 1937

the Nationalist Zone had been increased to 135,619 square miles, and a total population of 15,615,927 inhabitants, which was 70 per cent of Spain proper and 60 per cent of the population. Of the eleven towns in Spain of more than 100,000 inhabitants; namely, Madrid, Barcelona, Valencia, Seville, Bilbao, Malaga, Granada, Córdoba, Zaragoza, Murcia, Cartagena, six were under the jurisdiction of Generalissimo Franco's government (Seville, Malaga, Bilbao, Zaragoza, Córdoba, and Granada). Out of the fifty provincial capitals of Spain, thirty-five, or two thirds were under Nationalist rule, including Santa Cruz in Tenerife and Las Palmas de la Gran Canaria in the Canary Islands, and Palma de Majorca in the Balearic Islands. Franco's government was also in possession of the Spanish towns of Ceuta and Melilla in Africa as well as the Protectorate in Morocco, and the Spanish colonies in Ifni, Rio de Oro, the islands of the Gulf of Guinea, and on the mainlands of Muni in Africa, with an estimated area of 140,000 square miles. In short, the Nationalist Government controlled a grand total of 275,619 square miles, with the Barcelona-Valencia-Madrid government in control of 59,588 square miles. Strategically, Nationalist Spain, which embraced two thirds of the whole territory, held a definite advantage. She controlled the coal, iron, and steel, as well as the majority of essential foodstuffs, thus holding a decisive economic advantage as well. Life in Nationalist Spain was "as normal," wrote the London *Times,* April 1, 1937, "as life in England in 1915, or in any other country under such conditions. Business is organized, new industries spring up, the railway service functions normally and on seas communications are on a regular basis."

By the opening of the year 1938 life in Nationalist Spain had reached peace-time normality everywhere behind the eastern battle front. On January 31, General Franco reorganized the Nationalist Government on a peace-time basis with himself as President, and with a number of ministries

under him. Franco, himself, remained in supreme charge
of foreign affairs. General Jordana was made vice-president.
Six other main ministries and a secretariat were created.
The ministries thus established were, besides the Ministry
of Foreign Affairs, the ministries of Justice, Public Order,
Public Works, National Defense, Interior, and Finance. The
program of the new government of Nationalist Spain is set
forth in the following official proclamation to the Spanish
people issued from Burgos, February 7, 1938:

"On the occasion of its formation, the National Government proclaims its firm and sincere attachment to the Forces
on land, on sea, and in the air. This message of greeting is
addressed to all who make up those Forces — generals,
officers of all ranks, and the men of the Navy and the
Militias. It is certain that the first and principal care of this
Government, born of and during the war, must be to maintain the spiritual commonwealth of its warriors, united in
the determination to conquer.

"Let them rest assured that they are ever foremost in the
thoughts of the Government.

"This greeting is also for all who have shed their blood
for the cause, and those who have suffered bereavement;
those, too, who are taking part in this war on the enemy's
side, fighting in the midst of the error from which we shall
deliver them, firstly by force of arms and then by the truth
of our arguments. May the greeting of a Government, whose
first task is to put an end to the war by a decisive and lasting
victory, reach all those Spaniards who are taking part in
the struggle, and all those who, though far from Spain,
yet share our aspirations and our pride of race.

"After this most important task, the Government must
turn its attention to others.

"Firstly, the National-Syndicalist organization of the
State. All who are workers must be incorporated into this
organization in order that they may be made into a useful
instrument by which three groups — heads of concerns, tech-

nicians, and laborers, hitherto rivals — may be transformed into co-operators for the national good.

"The Press has one common spirit, and is learning to renounce the desire to be 'the fourth estate,' as also the idea of license of thought, which leads to abuses that caused the poisoning of the people's mind. The Press will be raised to serve the cause of truth in Spain.

"Another undertaking that the Government has in mind is the organization of a new municipal system, which will ensure healthy administration and good local government. It is of the greatest importance that short-sighted policies should be abandoned, and a genuine and reasonable national feeling fostered among our villages and hamlets.

"It is likewise necessary to embark upon the moral and material uplift of the whole Spanish nation. This will be achieved by means of a sound cultural and eugenic policy, which, carried out by our doctors and instructors, will do away with the ills which have attacked the soul and impaired the health of a people than which there is none finer.

"There are piles of debris which must be transformed into villages, churches, bridges, etc., to show that the Government's constructive revolutionary plans amount to something more than mere words. This side of national reconstruction must be given the careful attention that it deserves. Public works that are sources of wealth must be undertaken, in order to replace what has been destroyed by Asiatic madness, so that the standard of living may be raised among those who, in the slums and the hamlets, have not now the means of living decently.

"The Government will be mindful of the public servants, indispensable cogs in the machinery of civil administration, and give them that dignity which many deserve, and which all ought to deserve. They will be asked, in exchange for this, for scrupulous fulfillment of their duties and keenness. It will then be an honour to serve the State, just as it was in the finest periods of Spain's history.

"Our commercial policy will be regarded as of paramount importance, and our fiscal system will be upheld tenaciously, whilst in the sphere of economics — where Spain is giving to the world astonishing proof of her vigour and strength in maintaining enviable living conditions — it will be essential for all to have a true spirit of sacrifice in order to help on the reconstruction of our country.

"Spain is winning back for herself a great position in the world. Our foreign policy will be a policy of peace, but, let it be well understood, of peace compatible with the tremendous dignity of a people determined, by heroic warfare and an incomparable history, to gain the highest respect of all nations. This foreign policy, which will have the interests of the nation as its constant aim and contribution to the peace of Europe as its great desire, will be carried on by a people, which, in chivalrous fashion, will remember its friends of the days of its great struggle against the Communist menace directed against it by Russia. Our relations with the sister nations of South America will receive special attention, as also will the spiritual and material interests of the numerous Spaniards settled in their territories and of those who preserve the Spanish culture and language in the Far East.

"We shall ensure the reign of true justice, hallowed word which forms part of the threefold cry that accompanies our soldiers and which the Government representing them has today made its own: justice which makes this august mission something holy and incompatible with either weakness or despotism: justice which can be administered only by a true Government, which knows itself to be invested with complete authority and as free from demagogy as it is from frivolity.

"The importance of an agrarian policy must be realized. Firstly, because such is but just, and then because the excellent Spanish peasant deserves it after centuries of loyalty to Spain: an agrarian policy which will give to the country districts a fitting standard of living, by means of fair prices for its products, improvement of methods of cultivation, a national credit system and a better and fairer distribution of rural property.

"We must proclaim once more the profound sense of religious faith which has been the Spanish people's for all time, and which has imprinted itself on every chapter of their history. All the secular legislation, by which it was attempted to rob our country of its deep and robust Catholic sense, will be repealed speedily and thoroughly.

"Finally, there are several things which remain to be said to those who persist in treating with a Committee of Marxists, which in no way resembles a Government. All the cessions of territory, which are said to have been made or promised for the future, are purely imaginary. We shall win back our territory to the last inch, and also the whole of the property that has been taken from us.

"The task before the Government is immense, but it will be embarked upon at once with determination and tenacity. It is in silence that men work at difficult tasks, and it is in silence that we shall set about the solution of our problems. Little more remains to be said before this silence, which must never be interrupted except by realities. These are the words necessary to express the Government's firm loyalty to the Chief, Saviour of Spain: then other words to salute the nation. They could not be other than those words, ennobled with the blood of heroes and blackened by the powder of a thousand victories: '*Viva España! Arriba España!*'"[1]

During the winter of 1937 the war proceeded slowly, as both sides prepared for the 1938 spring offensive. Franco's activities were centered on strengthening the battle lines on the northeastern front extending from Huesca southward to Teruel. The lines around Madrid were quiet, as was the

---

[1] This English translation of the full text was published in *The Tablet*, London, February 12, 1938.

case in Andalusia. Franco's campaign was directed against the strategic military objectives only. A temporary Nationalist setback was the destruction and loss of Teruel on December 21, 1937. However, by February 19, 1938, Franco's soldiers were camped on all sides of the demolished city, and awaiting the white flag of surrender before trying to take it by storm. On February 22, his troops recaptured Teruel.

On March 9, Franco began his great offensive on the Aragon front in the effort to dismember the Barcelona-Valencia-Madrid government, and carry the war to a successful conclusion. In rapid succession Belchite, Caspe, Alcaniz, Fraga, and a number of other objectives were captured, advancing the Nationalist battle front to the Catalonian border in the northeast and to within forty miles of the Mediterranean Sea to the southeast. Meeting little resistance, Franco's armies pushed forward eighty miles on the Aragon front in less than three weeks. By the end of March, 1938, they reached Lérida, key city of Catalonia. Nothing was able to stay the relentless onslaught of Franco's advancing forces. Meanwhile the conquering march to the sea continued unabated. The way to victory lay open.

And Generalissimo Franco, the great campaigner of the Moroccan wars, was always in the vanguard, moving his base of operations as military strategy dictated, directing personally at the battle front the great drive which had as its objective the creating of a united and unified Spain.

Bibliographical Notes

Books, Official Records, Etc.:

José Montero y Aróstegui, *Historia y descripción de la ciudad y departamento naval de El Ferrol* (Madrid, 1859). An excellent history of El Ferrol, Franco's historic birthplace. For Franco's military career in Spanish Morocco, the following books, written by actual participants in the Moroccan wars, were used extensively: Dámaso Berenguer Fusté, *Campañas en el Riff y Yebala, 1921–1922. Notas y documentos de mi diario de operaciones* (Madrid, 1923); Francisco Franco, *Marruecos, Diario de una bandera* (Cuenca, 1922); Manuel Goded, *Marruecos, las etapas de la pacificación* (Madrid, 1932). The lengthy statement of Diego Hidalgo, ex-Minister of War, concerning Franco, which is quoted in Chapter XVI, is taken from Diego Hidalgo, *¿Por qué fuí lanzado del ministerio de guerra?* (Madrid, 1934). Other important sources specifically quoted or cited in the foregoing biography are: *Anuario militar* (Madrid, 1933), the official Spanish military register; *Diario de sesiones* (Madrid, 1936), the official journal of the Spanish parliament or cortes; Francisco Franco, "El merito en campaña," an unpublished article written by General Franco in 1921; José Moscardó, *Diario de operaciones* (Toledo, 1936); *La Gaceta,* Madrid, the official government daily news bulletin in which are published laws, regulations, etc. The last-named bulletin has been in the hands of the Madrid-Valencia-Barcelona government during the Spanish civil war.

NEWSPAPERS:

ABC, Madrid. Originally a conservative newspaper, *ABC* was taken over by the Syndicate of the Worker on July 18, 1936, and was converted into a Communist daily. *Claridad,* Madrid, an avowed Communist newspaper. *El Diario Vasco,* San Sebastián. In the early part of the civil war San Sebastián fell into the hands of the Madrid-Valencia-Barcelona government. Since the city has come under the jurisdiction of Franco's Nationalist government, *El Diario Vasco* has returned to its old, moderate, conservative character. *El Socialista,* Madrid, a Socialist paper. *La Nación,* Madrid. The building and the machinery of this newspaper were completely destroyed by fire at the beginning of the civil war. Other newspapers quoted or cited are: *Journal de Genève,* Geneva; *Le Matin,* Paris; *The Daily Express,* London; *The Times,* London; *The Tablet,* London.

Printed in the United Kingdom
by Lightning Source UK Ltd.
107910UKS00001B/58